RAQUEL WELCH

RAQUEL WELCH

SEX SYMBOL TO SUPER STAR

Peter Haining

ST. MARTIN'S PRESS

Library of Congress Cataloging in Publication Data
Haining, Peter.
   Raquel Welch: sex symbol to superstar
   1. Welch, Raquel.   2. Moving-picture actors and actresses—
United States—Biography.   I. Title.
   PN2287.W4557H3 1984   791.43′028′0924 (B)   84-17841

ISBN 0 312 663 96 X

First published in Great Britain by W. H. Allen & Co. Ltd.

First U.S. Edition

ACKNOWLEDGEMENTS

The author would like to thank the following for their help in
writing this book: Stephen Birmingham, John Robbins, Derek
Malcolm, Roderick Mann, Victor Davis, Donald Zec, Michael
Godwin, Nancy Mills, Michael Billington, Timothy Ferris, Jerry Le
Blanc, Bob Mills, Alexander Walker, Felix Barker, Arthur Knight,
Kenneth Bailey, Sheilah Graham, James Robert Parish, John
Russell Taylor, Clive Hirschhorn, George Melly, Mary Bredin,
David Leith and Fiona Macdonald Hull. Also *The New York Times*,
Playboy, *New York Post*, *The Hollywood Reporter*, *New York Daily News*,
Life, *Variety*, *Time*, *Paris Match*, *Rolling Stone*, *Penthouse*, *Show*, *ABC
Film Review*, *Look*, *Sunday Express*, *The Times*, *Daily Mail*, *Daily
Express*, *Daily Mirror*, *Sunday Times*, *Daily Telegraph*, *Village Voice*,
Cosmopolitan, *Newsweek*, *The Guardian*. And for photographs, Keystone
Press, Popperfoto, Paramount, 20th Century-Fox, Embassy
Pictures, MGM, Tigon Pictures, United Artists, Warner Bros and
American International Pictures. Colour section: pages 1, 2 and
4 – Camera Press (Terry O'Neill); page 3 – Kobal Collection.

'I don't know how to define my image as
a sex goddess, except that it connotates
flattery. It's also synonymous with not
being too bright. Well, I don't think I'm
an intellectual, whatever that is, but I
know I'm not dumb. I have a very organised,
analytical mind and I can do almost anything
I want to do if I put my mind to it.'

RAQUEL WELCH

Contents

The famous 'Cave Girl' poster
which made Raquel world-
famous

Introduction
The Dream Girl

RAQUEL WELCH IS one of the very few actresses who is recognised by her Christian name alone. That her spectacularly beautiful face and figure are instantly recognisable, too, goes without saying. Yet it is a rare accolade indeed that merely to say 'Raquel' in conversation is enough to identify her to anyone, anywhere in the world. It is an attribute that she shares with only a very few of this century's greatest stars – Marilyn, Brigitte and, of course, Garbo (though that was actually her invented surname).

In the almost twenty years since she became as much a part of the public consciousness as space travel, computers and the home video, Raquel has had a battle on her hands all the way. For if anyone has had to struggle to be considered a person and not just a symbol of male fantasy it is her. Remarkable as it may seem, Raquel was first dubbed a sex symbol as long ago as 1966 in one of her earliest films, *One Million Years BC*, and has carried the tag ever since – appearing in millions of pin-up photographs, featuring in countless jokes, and becoming the object of most men's sexual desire.

Even now, though, she says that after all she has done, achieved and *endured*, she has no illusions. 'I shall just be the sex symbol turned serious,' she says. 'To be a sex symbol is not to be a legitimate member of society. People are so hostile to you. They think you've been allowed to jump forward for less than legitimate reasons.' Then she sighs, 'But some people are meant to be the decorative things on the surface of the earth. Somebody's got to be the escape. But I don't think they want to know *me*. I'm a myth to them. If I were to go on stage and say, ''Hey, ladies and gentlemen, I washed the dishes myself this afternoon,'' they'd think, ''We don't want to know that.'' You must never try to be a real person.'

Whether one accepts that statement or not – and remember that it is both Raquel's critics as well as her admirers who have helped to establish her as one of the sex symbols of the sixties, seventies and eighties – she *is* a real person: beautiful, of course; determined, certainly; ambitious, naturally; at times brave; often vulnerable, as anyone in her chosen career invariably is, but above all, enduring.

Raquel's life story indeed bears eloquent testimony to the fact that only a survivor could have gone through what she has gone through and emerged having earned the accolade of super-star and remained sane. Stop to think for a moment of any other beautiful, highly-touted female actress of the sixties – even the seventies – who is still widely famous today, and when you have given up beyond one or two names, you will have some measure of her achievement.

It is an even more remarkable story when you consider that she has not lead a scandalous, immoral life to achieve notoriety; that she has *never* appeared naked on the screen (nor off it for that matter) nor taken part in any vicarious sex movies. Unlike many of the other so-called Hollywood beauty queens, she has only been married three times, and has raised two delightful children into well-balanced adults.

Raquel has, in fact, achieved her success in a climate of nudity being allowed for the first time in theatres, explicit, underground film-making coming into the open and stag hetero-sexual and homosexual movies gaining a kind of respectability by earning fortunes for their makers. As *Time* magazine had to admit in an article generally less than flattering about Raquel's ability, 'She has succeeded in becoming the No. 1 sex symbol in a world in which sex has been stripped of its last diaphanous shred of symbolism.'

She has also, of course, rarely been out of the news. She has been the object of innumerable headlines accusing her of fights, feuds and flare-ups of every conceivable kind. Yet, as she herself has often said, it has never seemed to matter who was right or wrong – it was always a better story for the press when Raquel Welch could be depicted as causing yet another fuss.

'I am totally vulnerable to anyone on a film set, to any secretary, even a salesgirl who wants to make a remark about me,' she says. 'I walk into a salon and anyone can ring a news-paper and say, "She's having a temper tantrum." I can't let it bother me, but it does each time.'

Her career has been a long one by Hollywood standards – by any standards in fact – and she can look back on it today with discernment and objectivity. 'When I started,' she says, 'I didn't know if I wanted to be a sex symbol or not, because I didn't know what one was. That's a media term. But from the time I was a child, I did want to be an actress who projected glamour and prettiness and sexiness.

'When I first started out, of course, I wasn't as good an actress as I am now. Believe me, I don't pooh-pooh the acting part, because that's terribly important, but I've always enjoyed the fact that I've been able to bring the glamour thing off.'

The woman who says these words is actually smaller than she appears on screen. She is medium height, at five foot six inches, and her figure is in proportion, rather than bosom-heavy as a million journalists and photographers have attempted to portray over the years. Meeting her, one is immediately struck by her physical *neatness*. Her face offset by rich, Titian-brown hair, has a *Latino* beauty: high cheekbones, large, dark brown eyes, a wide mouth with flashing white teeth, and a firm, well-defined jaw. Her nostrils may flare a little, but this is a face clearly made to photograph not just well, but superbly – as indeed is the rest of her body. Estimates of her figure vary from 37-22-35 to 40-24-36, yet aside from the bosom which only a blind man could resist observing, she has equally striking long legs and the rounded thighs of a dancer. When she walks, she moves lithely and gracefully. There is, indeed, such a sense of natural rightness about Raquel that one immediately begins to doubt all those stories about her having plastic surgery and silicone injections.

'I'm supposed to be some kind of walking, talking doll,' she has protested on many an occasion, 'you know, silicone from head to foot. But how can I disprove it? Perhaps I should let people try the squeeze test!'

She also knows that some people are disappointed when they meet her. They have read all about this incredibly sexy creature and expect extraordinary things of her. 'But,' she says, 'the whole sex goddess thing is rather limiting. I often feel apologetic about the whole thing. It's not a sympathetic position to be in, except when something tragic happens to you, the way it did to Marilyn. Women think of you as a threat. Everybody believes you have occult powers over the opposite sex, which is ridiculous. They feel that a sex goddess is a lot less deserving of fame and financial success than someone who is notable for acting ability. In fact, some people are even apologetic about being attracted to a film star who is known mostly for her looks. Marilyn had the same problem. I always liked her, but I didn't think she could act her way out of a paper bag. Her success came too late in her career for it to be really satisfying. And she carried around a terrible inferiority complex Hollywood instilled in her when she was trying to get a foothold for herself.'

To admirers of Marilyn Monroe such remarks may well border on the sacrilegious, but Raquel, who talks easily and fluently in a discerning and intelligent way, also knows that her tongue can run away with her. She says with disarming candour: 'I have a terrible mouth that gets me in a lot of trouble. I really do. Sometimes I say things I'm really sorry for. When I get short-tempered – and my temper can be short – then my mouth goes off, and later I regret it. That's one of my worst faults, I think.' Knowing some of the ordeals she has had to face, I find it difficult not to be sympathetic with someone who can be *that* honest.

Those who know Raquel intimately say she has very little ego; that she is not one for putting on airs and graces like many actors do when they have a captive audience; and that she displays sound commonsense and holds strong and obviously well thought-out opinions – not the least important of these being about her own profession. 'I think that anybody who's in a creative field is syphoning off all the things that interest him,' she says. 'Artists are always observing. They're voyeurs. At least to a certain degree. I think that as the moment happens they are storing up the memory of it for their repertoire of experience which they can draw on, professionally. Actors, actresses, directors, writers. They all do it. It makes us a weird group of people. The average person, hearing me say that, might think of artists as people spying on life. But you can't write or create anything you haven't experienced. What can you bring to art except what you've experienced and observed?'

Her friends say that Raquel also has a fine sense of humour which is actually at its best when she is entertaining quietly at

The price of fame – forever surrounded by the world's pressmen

home. Though she does go to fashionable parties occasionally, she prefers intimate dinners or just relaxing by reading, writing letters to friends, watching movies (she admires Cary Grant, Richard Gere and Dudley Moore among male actors, and Diane Keaton and Meryl Streep as actresses) or listening to music (Leon Russell is a favourite). She loves travelling, too, which is perhaps just as well for someone with her career. 'I suppose I'm really quite ordinary in my private life,' she says with a smile.

People who only know of Raquel through those millions of pin-ups which still adorn the walls of factories and offices around the world, and through a few of her earlier, lightweight films, tend to forget that she is one of the very few Hollywood stars (Liza Minnelli is another) who appears not only in movies, but on the stage and in television as well. Most movie stars, glamour queens in particular, tend to stick to the big screen, and if they do attempt the other mediums, usually do so with a notable lack of success. Raquel has never been afraid of testing her talent in the entertainment world beyond films, nor has she worried – as others might – that by accepting less money from stage or television work, this would affect her salary demands for movies. To her, the challenge has been all important – buttressed, it must be said out of fairness, by extraordinary financial returns from her pictures, good, bad or indifferent.

There are those who will claim of Raquel that she owes everything to the brilliantly orchestrated picture and publicity campaign that her second husband, Patrick Curtis, ran for her. That it was this debut on the printed page before she had ever been seen on the screen that made her name. Certainly, she was heralded as a new sensation – 'The Girl of Tomorrow', 'The Most Exciting Star since Marilyn Monroe' and 'A Girl in a Million' – before cinema audiences saw her act. But in the final analysis, publicity can do no more than get an actress known – she must ultimately deliver the goods to the paying customers or else face the inevitable oblivion which has claimed countless others. The number of would-be sex symbols of the past twenty years is legion; millions of dollars of studios' money has gone into promoting young hopefuls who, when brought before the all-seeing eye of the camera, have failed.

Yet not so with Raquel. She has become one of the most talked-about, photographed, filmed and successful box-office attractions of the second half of the century. She has been described as the logical successor to Jean Harlow, Rita Hayworth, Jane Russell and Marilyn Monroe in the sex symbol stakes (though she herself now has what she considers welcome challengers for the role), yet, unlike them, she has displayed a far wider range of talent and still has much of her career before her. Like her predecessors, though, she was well aware that the Hollywood moguls wanted her to conform to an image, to become the symbol for voluptuous and vicarious screen excitement, but she has resisted this pressure with determination. Back in 1969 she declared, 'I feel people are trying to bury me in a sea of C-cups. Marilyn couldn't fight it because she wasn't strong enough. But I think I can lick it.'

This book traces the eventful years of Raquel's life from sex goddess to superstar. It is the story of a beautiful young girl who dreamed of being a movie star, tried to get a break as a starlet in Hollywood, had to become a cheesecake queen in Europe to gain recognition, and then had to fight the studio executives to become accepted as an actress. It is also the story of a girl who

14

had faith in her own ability and who insisted steadfastly on controlling her own destiny. 'I was given a marvellous body,' she says without a trace of false modesty. 'I have exploited being a sex symbol as well as being exploited as one. I have no regrets.'

Her life today takes her from her flat in Central Park West, New York, where she lives with her third husband, Frenchman André Weinfeld, to Paris, where they have an apartment and also to Los Angeles where for years she has had a palatial two-storey colonial house with a pool standing on a picturesque three-and-a-half acre estate in Benedict Canyon. And, of course, wherever her next film, televison spectacular or concert appearance demands, tackling each with the equanimity that the past forty-three years of her life have finally brought her.

'I don't know that I have a philosophy of life,' she says, 'but one thing that I learned recently is not to be afraid to be afraid. There will be frightening and painful things in my life, and if I accept that I'll be afraid – and there's nothing wrong with being afraid – then it helps a great deal.

'Some people try to avoid being afraid all the time. They can never come to grips with different points in their lives which could be important transitions for them. It's always frightening to do anything a little bit different.

'Somehow I find it better for me to admit that here comes that nice familiar feeling of fear.'

She knows, too, that she is never going to lose her image. 'I like to have a good time with it,' she says, 'but I still get very frightened that everybody will think I'm just a vapid sex symbol. We need people to escape into fantasy worlds, though. We need dream girls. I like being a dream girl, but I'm a real girl too.'

And, indeed, in the pages which follow I have tried to write the story of a girl who became a dream girl and yet through everything has remained a real girl, too.

1 Birdlegs in Fantasyland

THE COASTLINE OF California is one of the most beautiful
stretches of ochre sands and azure blue water to be found anywhere in the world. Even if the sprawling cities of San Francisco,
Los Angeles and San Diego may offend the aesthetic eye, there
is still much on this coast to stir up dreams of paradise. The
people, too – the deep-tanned, voluptuous women and athletic,
blond men – with their laid-back lifestyle matched by a desire to
find the promise of tomorrow, today, have given the West Coast
of America an aura which goes far beyond any pictures painted
by its most famous colony, Hollywood. For California *is* the
place of dreams; it *is* the land where fantasy can become reality.

It was to this coast that two-year-old Jo-Raquel Tejada was
brought in 1942 by her mother and father from the windy city of
Chicago where she had been born on 5 September 1940. The
family came to settle in La Jolla, which is just north of San
Diego, the third largest of the Pacific Coast cities, and only a few
miles from Tijuana which marks the border between the United
States and Mexico. Although one of California's oldest settle-
ments, San Diego is famous for its landlocked natural harbour
which is home to the US Navy's largest fleet, the Eleventh, as
well as having become identified with research into oceanics and
aerospace.

La Jolla, by contrast, is a resort town which has developed
into a pretty if somewhat plasticised community since it first
became a get-away-from-it-all spot for the San Diego residents
in 1886. It is strung along five miles of beautifully protected
beach, with the gentle surf at La Jolla Cove attracting swimmers
and divers as well as skin and scuba divers who find endless
pleasure in the clear water and undersea 'gardens'. Perhaps,
though, the greatest attraction are the caves, situated just off
Coast Boulevard, which have with good reason been compared
to the grottos on the Isle of Capri. The view of La Jolla Bay from
the bluff just above the cave entrance underlines still further the
magic of this coast.

The Tejada family moved into a modest one-storey stucco
house with an asphalt shingle roof just two blocks from Wind
and Sea Beach. From here, across the neat front lawn with its
pepper tree, little Raquel could gaze out to sea and the rolling

*A young girl dreaming of
stardom...*

17

breakers which provide one of the most testing surfing areas on the West Coast. But the sea was not to prove where her dreams lay . . .

Raquel's father, Armand C. Tejada, emigrated to the United States from his native Bolivia, though his family was originally of Castilian extraction. (The name Tejada is said to have been given to the family by a medieval Spanish king and means 'spears of clay'.) In America, Armand studied at the University of Illinois and qualified as a structural-stress engineer. While at the university, he met Josephine Sarah Hall, a dark-haired, pretty girl of English-Scottish descent and they got married. Armand thereafter worked for a short while in Chicago, before obtaining a somewhat better job at General Dynamics' La Jolla plant and consequently moving himself, his wife and his little daughter to the West Coast. In La Jolla, the Tejada's were to have two more children, a boy and a girl.

The very different natures of her parents were to have contrasting effects on Raquel, as she was to observe later in her life: 'Like most actresses, I'm fragmented inside,' she said. 'There are so many people inside me, crying to get out. My father was very Latin around the edges, from Spain, and my mother's family comes from England, so I have this passionate side to me and also a conservative side. Some mixture!'

The little girl was brought up strictly. She went in awe of her father and was early taught by her mother about morals and propriety. 'I think women of my generation often looked up to their mothers and regarded them very affectionately,' she says today, 'but at the same time they wondered: "Do I want to make all the same sacrifices?" My mother was what I call perfect. In everything she did she was nurturing us. She worked because the family needed the income. She was a statistical clerk at the Convair aircraft factory. She used to get up at 5 a.m. and take the bus. She'd have set out breakfast for us. Every night she'd come home and cook dinner and wash the clothes and bake. She always seemed so tired to me. I don't want to paint any terrible pictures of her because she was, and is, a very strong lady in her way, and she's still very energetic. She's undauntingly optimistic in her outlook. But I always thought: "My God, how do you do all of that?'' She was always so sweet with us. And I just thought that was too much. She was doing too much for us.'

Although Raquel had the pleasures of the beach and the ocean to fill her childhood days, because her parents were so busy at their jobs she began to live more and more within herself. 'When I was a child I was happiest in fantasy,' she recalls. 'I wasn't good at dealing with reality. Telephone poles and the rest spoiled things. I wanted things to be perfect. I wanted a storybook life, to be Rapunzel and Cinderella and Sleeping Beauty, all the beautiful ladies that wonderful men came along on their big white horses and dragged away. Which is not remarkable, a lot of kids grow up that way. But I decided it was gonna happen. Go for broke, honey, guts up all the way.'

One area of escape that Raquel discovered when she was very small was music. Her parents were record collectors and she loved to spend hours listening to the tunes they bought. Although the early forties were very much the era of crooners – Frank Sinatra in particular was sending the nation's bobbysoxers into ecstasy – it was the voice of Al Jolson that caught Raquel's ear. 'I particularly liked him,' she recalls, 'and in no time I had memorised all his numbers.'

Another significant moment occurred when she was five. She was chosen to recite 'The Night Before Christmas' at the local church where she had also started to sing in the choir. 'That was when I first realised I enjoyed performing,' she recalls. Two years later Raquel was given a tiny acting part in a San Diego Junior Theatre production of *The Princess and the Caterpillar*. It was not a very auspicious stage debut, though, for as she remembers she was cast as a boy!

That same year, too, she began to discover something that was to be even more significant in her life – the movies. There was one picture in particular that had an immediate effect on her. 'What happened was I saw the film *Red Shoes*,' she says. 'Not once, but ten times. I decided then I wanted to be a ballerina.'

Raquel's father had always been very keen on self-improvement and on a number of occasions talked about her having ballet lessons to give her poise. Now, she jumped at the chance. For the next seven years, in fact, Raquel took lessons from a local instructor, Irene Isham Clark, formerly with the San Francisco Opera Company, whose studio looked out over La Jolla Cove. Still tanned and lithe, but now grey-haired, Irene Clark remembers her former pupil very well. 'Raquel has the same drive as those people who came over here from Europe with a recipe for chocolate and $200 and become millionaires. They have a dream that doesn't leave them. The first time I ever saw her she was a fifth-grader. She came home to play with my daughter. She was extremely vibrant. You *remembered* her. Precise. Not overpowering, but a positive little personality. She had plenty of aptitude for the dance, but there was no humility in her approach to art. She enjoyed attention too much, and she knew how to get it.'

The 'little personality' had, though, come to realise that this dream, too, had its drawbacks. 'I realised it would have meant keeping my toe in a resin box most of the time, and I didn't have the dedication or the self-discipline for that.'

Red Shoes was not the only film Raquel saw at La Jolla's one movie house during the late forties which left an impression on her. She was entranced by the fantasy world of *The Prince of Foxes* and very impressed by the acting of Laurence Olivier in *Hamlet*. Dan Dailey musicals set her toes tapping, and she went into ecstasy like many of her girlfriends over the handsome movie stars John Derek and Tony Curtis.

With each passing year, in fact, she became more sure of what she *really* wanted to be – as she told Nancy Mills in 1978: 'I have had this romance with films and performing ever since I was a child. I wanted to be an actress since I was seven. To me it was a very special, privileged world where you got to be a child all your life. You could always pretend to be someone you weren't. It gave you a licence to do a lot of things you'd never do in real life.

'I always had this vision. Part of it came from my father's very exacting, critical view of me all through my early child-hood. I felt that I wanted to prove to him that I could be some-body special.'

She elaborated further to Michael Billington: 'I never wanted to be a nurse or a social worker, but coming from a town without any theatre, I got involved with movies early on: they became the source of my fantasies and I created my own little world around them. I was also sent to ballet classes, chiefly so that I should keep out of trouble: people would pat you on the head and say that at least you weren't getting into bad ways by going down to the beach with all those boys. What they didn't know was who picked you up after ballet classes.'

It was also evident that Raquel was changing dramatically in her appearance as she reached her teens – in particular when she entered La Jolla High School. Her nose had always had a high Latin ridge which gave it a rather unattractive look, while her legs were so thin she was known among her friends – affectionately, let it be said – as 'Birdlegs'. Now, though, her figure suddenly began to develop.

Talking to Timothy Ferris in August 1974 she recalled this time of change very clearly: 'In high school I was "Rocky", then after the equipment arrived, "Hotrocks". I suddenly got a lot of attention from the guys. I was Miss La Jolla and a cheerleader. We were young girls with new equipment, struttin' our stuff. I was liking it but it was a little confusing, because high school boys are trying to find out a few things themselves, you know, and it's very dodgy. Push a little, shove a little . . .

'My father was also very tough on me, though I tried to please him, got lots of good grades and everything. But when puberty arrived and people started to say, "My, aren't you pretty!", it was almost too late. I had almost built into myself by then that I would never get the acceptance I needed from my father. I was on the defensive. I still have that with me now, to a degree.

'Beauty to me is a crutch. It's what I built my career on. To be accepted by other human beings was always my first insecurity, and all the things I tried to do in childhood were eventually solved when I got to the age that I could be accepted as a woman. When the equipment arrived, about age fourteen, that was how I first knew people liked me. Up until that time I was really quite frightened that people didn't like me at all.

What I'm saying is, when I turned out to have a nice figure and be a pretty girl, at least that was one area I could succeed in. Do you see? At least a little light shone down.'

If Raquel felt a lack of self-confidence – even though she was so evidently developing into a beauty – she faced her phobia in the most positive way: by taking on parts in the school plays and by entering local beauty contests. 'One year at school,' she recalls with a smile, 'I did a take-off of Jane Russell from the film *Gentlemen Prefer Blondes*, singing the ''Is Anyone Here for Love'' number. I wore high heels and black tights and was stuffed to the hilt with padding!'

There was no padding required when it came to beauty contests, however, and Raquel won her first local contest in the summer just before she was fourteen! She had been persuaded to enter the contest to find 'Miss Photogenic' by some of her friends. She beat 150 other girls. 'I was thrilled,' she recalled later. 'I don't think I'd ever wanted anything as much as I did to win that beauty contest.'

The following year, aged fifteen, she was the youngest ever winner of the beauty contest to find 'Miss La Jolla' held in conjunction with the Ramona Pageant, of which Victor Jory was the annual director. She also became a cheerleader at school and was vice-president of her graduating class.

One beauty contest success led to another, and she successively became 'Miss San Diego', 'Miss Contour' and 'Maid of California'. A bigger triumph still was winning the title 'Fairest of the Fair', of which the organiser, Don Diego was to remark later: 'There were prettier girls around, but none had her figure or her drive. Most girls tremble before they get on stage. Raquel never did. You could tell by the way she got up there that she *was* the queen.'

Despite these achievements, Raquel was neither swept off her feet nor made to feel very special by those around her. 'No one ever fawned over me,' she says. 'Do you think in my day-to-day life that my mother, my friends, even a boy would tell me I was attractive all the time? Oh, no, it would have been too much for his masculine pride. I entered those beauty contests just for fun. I didn't think I'd win. Well, I did. I'll tell you why I won –

An early modelling pose

because I *walked* the best in high heels. Not because I was beautiful. The others didn't know how to walk. *Well*, do you suppose all the girls gathered round me when I won a beauty contest? No, it was not fun and games when I was growing up.'

By the time she was sixteen, however, there was no denying that Raquel Tejada had blossomed into a striking, long-limbed beauty. She weighed 118 pounds, was five foot six inches tall, and had a most appealing chestnut touch in her hair. She wore a sweater well and her shapely legs and bottom turned many a head. Only her blunt nose marred what one writer called 'the hauntingly exquisite beauty of a young Ava Gardner'.

At this time, too, Raquel had also determined what *kind* of actress she was going to be. 'I knew I wanted to be an actress who projected glamour and prettiness and sexiness,' she said. And she also felt she wanted to put some of the experience she had been gaining out of school into use. For she had spent much of her spare time as an apprentice at the La Jolla Playhouse, attending workshop classes and learning all about the theatre from scene-painting to understudying the lead roles. She had even been given a few small parts in some of the Playhouse productions, including a number of her own in *Pal Joey*. She had also worked with other community theatre projects in San Diego and the Drury Lane Players in La Jolla where she had a little foretaste of what was to come when she portrayed a sexy dancer in a musical review called *Caribbean Holiday*.

But two events conspired almost at once to put a temporary halt to her acting plans. First, her parents were divorced. Secondly, she fell headlong into marriage with a class-mate, James Welch.

Even with the passage of time, she recalls the break-up of her parents' marriage, and the effect it had upon her, with great clarity. 'My folks got divorced after many long years of being together,' she says. 'I understood what was going on at a very young age. I knew whether there was a happy atmosphere or not. I don't think it's necessary any more to have a traditional home in the old-fashioned sense where you had father and mother through a lifetime, for better or worse. Don't you think everybody feels rotten if they find out their folks have made some great unhappy sacrifice for them? I think it gives a child much more of a guilt feeling to learn that he was part of something that was unpleasant and that had made his parents unhappy.'

Raquel has also been equally frank about how she got into her first marriage when she was just sixteen. She and handsome, curly-haired James Westley Welch had been dating ever since she had entered La Jolla High School in 1954. He was the stepson of the founder of the Fed Mart Corporation, America's largest discount chain, and from his early teens had displayed a strong streak of rebelliousness, preferring tattered jeans, a sweatshirt and rubber sandals to any kind of regular clothes. Jim also loved the sea and was never happier than when off sailing – particularly on board tuna fishing expeditions that worked off the South American coast, staying away sometimes for months on end. In fact he dropped out of high school in his senior year to follow this urge.

Although Raquel felt he was irresponsible, she could not control what was happening to her. 'I was swept up in this emotion of having the great Prince Charming love of my life,' she says. 'I remember I used to put on plays in my garage. Fairytales. *Snow White.* Those simple little stories where good prevails over evil and every little girl dreams she is Snow White. She is a lovely little creature pursued by a big, evil monster intent on killing her but always stopped by the Prince Charming who loves her because she is sweet and nice. I had a very middle-class idea of the way things should be. It starts out in bliss, but it doesn't turn out that way. Your high school sweetheart doesn't have a real vocation and is not ready to support a wife and children. And he isn't valiant in facing all the problems that come up. But he was so terrific-looking. I had the female vanity of thinking I could fix anything wrong with him. But he couldn't be changed – mostly because he was off on tuna clippers, making some kind of a living. Sometimes he was gone three months at a whack.'

During the early years of her film career, Raquel was very reluctant to talk about this first marriage, but recently she has been able to view it more objectively, all the more so because James Welch has also spoken frankly about their time together and his part in its failure. Talking in 1973 to Jerry Le Blanc in San Diego where he is now president of a million-dollar conglomerate, Welch said: 'It has been said that our marriage was brutal, extremely unpleasant and unhappy, and I admit I was a bastard to Raquel a lot of the time. But I'm telling you it was also happy, beautiful, even idyllic at times. I won't say anything about Raquel. We loved each other then. It was a long time ago, but when I think back, I've really got to hand it over to her in a way. She had guts. There I was forever off on a tuna boat and she didn't even know when I would be back. But she waited for me. We were just kids in love.'

Raquel takes up the story here: 'I had to find work, because we needed the money. I had a state college scholarship in theatre arts in San Diego. But all this went down the tube when I started to have babies. There must have been some contraceptives around at that time, but I didn't know about them – I was such a little nit. After my son Damon was born in 1959, I tried to hold down all my units in school, as well as work, and take care of Damon. I had a job on a TV talk show in the morning at $7.50 a show, and I modelled in department stores. I already had enough responsibility for a grown woman, and I was getting sick all the time. I was so innocent and small-town. On the TV job, the producer told me, confidentially, I didn't have to join the union and pay a big fee. So they never paid me scale for the work I did, and I was too dumb to know better. It was really illegal. I think my small-townness still follows me around. I still need somebody to bring down the axe; somebody to say, "Oh, no, she's not going to do that."'

One of Raquel's early jobs would have ensured her a little piece of immortality, for while she was working as secretary to a bishop in San Diego she was seen by a sculptor who specialised in religious statues. He was instantly struck by her beauty and asked her to pose for a stone statue he was about to carve. The extra money appealed to Raquel and she agreed. Hence, today, her likeness in the modest robes of the Virgin Mary looks down from a building in the centre of San Diego.

Raquel's television job in San Diego was on the *Sun-Up* programme in which she gave out the weather, did occasional interviews and commercials and sometimes modelled the latest fashions. This lead to some modelling work for Toni Tacoma, the West Coast co-ordinator for the May Company stores, as well as a considerable amount of photographic work. 'I turned to modelling because I hoped to become an actress and thought that I could get to New York and model there until I got an acting break,' Raquel said later. Her photograph did, though, begin to appear with increasing frequency in local papers and magazines.

There are those who claim to have worked with Raquel at this period of her life who maintain that her breasts were not as big as when she became famous, although these people have all agreed she had poise, a beautiful complexion and a great presence. Bob Mills, a TV colleague in 1961, claimed in 1979: 'I'll be generous and say she was a thirty-four-inch bust. She really was rather flat-chested. She was terribly sensitive about her poor bust and the guys used to joke about it. If only they'd known then where her future lay . . .'

Raquel, as we shall see later, has always steadfastly denied she has ever had her figure altered by cosmetic surgery, but it remains a regrettable fact that what has almost amounted to an obsession among many journalists with her breasts has too often obscured fair and objective reporting of her talent. The evidence of her childhood photographs make it clear, however, that remodelling work was carried out on her nose at some time, probably a little later when she was working in Dallas, according to her former mother-in-law.

Although he was away a good bit of the time, James Welch was full of praise for Raquel as a housewife. He recalls that she was a good cook and worked hard to keep their little apartment at Pacific Beach spic and span, humming and dancing to Elvis Presley tunes as she did her chores. But all the outside work Raquel Welch – as she was now known – was getting, such as television spots, photographic engagements and modelling, did not help their relationship. There were rows, and the couple even separated for a time.

Welch particularly remembers a party at Del Mar to which they had both been invited after she had won a beauty contest.

He found himself pushed to one side while Raquel was swept into the limelight. 'Christ, I couldn't even get close enough to *talk* to her,' he recalls. 'I couldn't handle that sort of thing for very long. Up until that point I thought I could share a life with her. But I began to realise that we would never make it.'

Raquel herself, though, was also feeling the pressure of this lifestyle as she admitted in 1972. 'I became more and more ill,' she said, 'psychosomatically ill. It wasn't all my husband's fault. It was just me – being married too young, getting pregnant, worrying about money, that kind of thing. All of that put together affected me. I lost weight. I couldn't move quickly. My vision became fuzzy. All that began to scare me to death. My doctor recommended a hypnotherapist, who was a regular MD who used hypnosis on people and who didn't believe in anaesthesia for operations. My doctor thought hypnosis would be the most direct way to root out the cause of my hysteria. I was sceptical but I was desperate. Then I began to discover, through hypnosis, what some of these stresses were that made me feel so bad; the things *not* on the surface that immobilised me. After several sessions, I began to get better and I got hold of myself for the first time since my marriage. These particular problems have never occurred again.'

Jim Welch did make an attempt to save his marriage, promising to spend more time at home with Raquel. And what happened? 'The first thing I knew I was pregnant again,' Raquel continues. 'Did he do this deliberately to keep me in my place and make me stay home? Was I too balky a female? The second pregnancy was not an easy one for me and again he wasn't around to help too much. All of my activities were confined to going from one crib to the other with odd modelling jobs and the little TV job on the side. I decided I wasn't going to have three babies in this same situation. After three and a half years, I knew the only way to leave my husband was to get out of town. I had to vanish. And I did.'

Raquel's second pregnancy in fact forced her to quit her job at the TV station, and her baby was born the day after Christmas in 1961. The child, a girl, was named Tahnee, after Jim's mother. Welch takes up the story: 'After Tahnee was born I took

one last thirty-day fishing job – mostly to clear my head and think things out. When I got back I realised I was still very much in love with Raquel. But it was obviously over. The competition was insane. Once, just to keep up with her, I actually jumped into the bullring at Tijuana. Don't ask me what I was trying to prove. She won't agree with me, but it was my idea to end it. I know she was seriously considering the same thing. I probably beat her to the punch by about six months.'

What is beyond dispute is that the couple parted and later their marriage was dissolved. Their respective assessments of their time together have been vividly expressed. 'It was stupid to have got married that first time,' Raquel told *Penthouse* magazine in 1972. 'I was sixteen and he was eighteen. Just because we admired each other's looks. It was a marriage based on nothing.'

'Unlike Raquel,' James Welch told *Show* magazine in 1970, 'I look back on our marriage with fondness, even though it has haunted me. I've stayed away from La Jolla. I've stayed away from friends. But you can never get divorced from Raquel Welch.'

In fact, the only thing that remains of their marriage *is* the name that Jim Welch gave Raquel: the name which she has chosen to retain for her professional career and which has become famous way beyond anything its original owner might have imagined!

The taste of public acclaim, modest though it might have been, decided Raquel on her next course of action. She would work her way to New York, break into the theatre world there, and then progress to Hollywood on a crest of critical acclaim. It seemed so natural and so inevitable. 'I first thought of going to New York,' Raquel recalls. 'I had a school friend there, studying at the Juilliard. He wrote me terrific postcards saying how full of vitality New York is, how it's fun even to be down-and-out in New York because there you have a real life with a capital L. I decided to go, but my mother said, "Well, I think that's a terribly rough place to be with two little babies, Raquel," and that slowed me down a bit. Then, somebody at the store where I modelled talked with Nieman-Marcus in Dallas and they offered me a job and I accepted. I was so

2 Svengali and The Cheesecake Queen

THE RAQUEL WELCH who arrived in Hollywood in 1963 cherished the same dream as a million beautiful girls before her. And like them, too, she hoped for the same golden future at the end of the celluloid rainbow. Although she believed implicitly in her dream, she was under no illusions about the obstacles which faced her. 'When I came to Hollywood,' she recalled recently, 'I had no more experience than that of a naïve little small-town girl diligently pursuing a hobby.'

Perhaps not surprisingly, considering their attitudes, Raquel's parents did not share her ambition, and she vividly recalls a scene with her mother before she left La Jolla. 'My mother took a dim view of what I wanted to do,' she recalls. 'One day she threw at me a copy of *The Carpetbaggers* by Harold Robbins. ''Read this,'' she said, ''and tell me if that really is the kind of career that you want.'' I read it avidly from start to finish.

'It was a tremendous help to me because from it I learned what *not* to do. I made up my mind that Hollywood is not a place filled with sinister characters lurking in half-shadows waiting to seduce virgins. It's a place filled with hard-headed business people out to make money.'

Raquel's father feared for his beautiful daughter, too, though he knew it would be impossible to stop her. 'I had a very puritan upbringing because my father was a Bolivian immigrant,' she was to say in 1978. 'He never liked my being a sex symbol. He always said I should have studied Shakespeare. But I always thought it was great fun to strut my stuff.'

The girl who stepped from the plane at Los Angeles was still far from being a sex symbol, however, though her striking good looks did catch the eye of one man – as Raquel likes to recall in a story she told *ABC Film Review* in September 1969. 'I had no sooner arrived at the airport,' she said, 'than a man ran up to me saying that his name was Leonard Weinrib and he was doing a television show at the airport and would like me to appear in it. ''Hollywood has been waiting for you,'' he said. It seemed such an obvious hoax – almost like something out of *The Carpetbaggers* – that I just brushed him off and hurried on my way because I had to find some place to live. I later discovered that his name *was* Lennie Weinrib, he *was* doing a television show at the airport and he *did* want me to appear in it!'

If Raquel ever thought for a moment that such an incident might be an omen of what was to come, she did not have time to dwell on the matter as she got on with the business of trying to survive in the city which had broken so many screen-struck girls. The failure rate certainly did not deter her any more than it has done any other young hopeful, but her resolve was certainly tested to the utmost.

First, she had to find somewhere for herself and her two young children, Damon and Tahnee, to live. Her scant resources, augmented solely by a meagre allowance from Jim Welch who was by then doing his military service as a Green Beret in Vietnam, only enabled her to take a seventy-dollar-a-month apartment. Then came the business of getting work. With no car, she had to make the best of the city's transport system as she began the arduous business of trying to establish herself.

She demonstrated her resourcefulness by signing up with an agent, Noel Marshall, who, sensing her potential, began to coach her in the fundamentals of studio saleswomanship. Every day she got up at 6 a.m., dropped the children off at a day care centre, and set off making the rounds of photographers and modelling agencies. She did get some work modelling for a dress manufacturer, but more often was in one queue or another trying to get a shot at film-making.

Like any would-be actress with a beautiful face and figure, Raquel received 'offers' from certain of the shadier characters on the fringes of Hollywood. Her anger still rises today at the memory of certain producers she encountered who made it quite plain they picked their actresses by the old 'casting couch' method. 'To me, it was an outright insult that these men should turn a professional casting interview into a seduction or proposition session,' she says. 'I never once "teased" my way into an interview. They'd just assume you know, big producer, little starlet who'd do anything for a break. It hardens you. A girl has to be tough to go through that. It screwed me up – my attitude – for years.'

Friends who remember Raquel from these years are full of praise for her determination and refusal to allow herself to be compromised. On top of the endless trudging from agency to photographer to film studio and back again, she also did a tremendous amount of working out in the gym or at home to keep herself fit and her figure in good shape.

At night, though, she was glad to seek the sanctuary of her little apartment. 'When I first got to Hollywood,' she says, 'I was sufficiently scared after my Dallas experiences that, after looking for work all day, I wouldn't see or talk to anybody or go out at all. I locked the door and stayed home every night, and that was it. A lot of men were looking me over, and probably thought I was a small-town easy mark, very vulnerable. When they find out you're a woman living alone, they can cause you bad trouble, coming around, being awful. These are the men who won't take no for an answer. You can't get rid of them. They harass you and wait in front of your building and you don't know what to do. If you didn't answer the phone or the doorbell they'd find something to bash through the glass. I was always moving with my kids in the dark of the night. I found that men can be pretty tough.'

With the passing weeks and months it began to look increasingly as if she was going nowhere: as if the dream was turning sour. Destitution seemed to be staring Raquel in the face, and she admits that it was only the kindness of certain friends who saw her and her young children through some of the really black days.

Then little rays of hope began to brighten her horizon. Her persistent knocking on the doors of the talent agencies landed her tiny parts in television shows such as *The Virginian*, *McHale's Navy*, *The Rogues*, and *Wendy and Me*. Then came a regular spot on the weekly ABC television show, *Hollywood Palace* in which she was a 'Billboard Girl' who announced the stars and the various other acts on the variety show. And this, in its turn, led to three appearances on the top-rated Danny Kaye show, and several bookings for the Red Skelton programme.

Next came her first film break – a three-day acting job in an Elvis Presley film called *Roustabout* made by Paramount in the summer of 1964 and directed by Hal B. Wallis. Although Raquel was fully aware of Presley's music, she did not count herself a particular fan – although this was the small part she was cast to play in the film. During the course of what is a rather banal picture in which Presley plays a wandering tough guy who joins a travelling carnival, Raquel made a fleeting appearance as an eighteen-year-old college student who stood looking suitably entranced as Elvis went through one of his musical numbers. The rock'n'roller certainly emerged with no particular credit from the movie – only his co-star the redoubtable Barbara Stanwyck received any kind of favourable comment – and Raquel herself perhaps fortunately received no screen credit whatsoever.

From a fresh-faced young college student, Raquel made the unlikely though more demanding step to playing a call girl in her next assignment in Joseph E. Levine's production of *A House Is Not A Home*. Based on the autobiography of New York's most famous madam, Polly Adler (played by Shelley Winters), Raquel was one of 'Polly's Girls' in a picture which despite the interest and challenge of its story matter, came across as rather pedestrian and unappealing. It was released in August 1964 to almost universally poor reviews. Raquel received the princely fee of $300 for her contribution.

Another walk-on part in *Do Not Disturb*, a lack-lustre story with Doris Day and Rod Taylor as a couple comically attempting infidelity to revive their rather staid marriage, proved the third in a trio of films that did nothing for Raquel's embryo career, other than give her some much needed work and a little taste of the business of film-making. But the determined little girl from La Jolla could at least feel she had her feet on the bottom rung of the show business ladder. All the more so when *Life* magazine in its issue of 2 October 1964 featured a photo story on up-and-coming Hollywood starlets – among whom were Raquel and a certain Mia Farrow.

Her confidence took a further boost on 21 November when she was invited to the Twelfth Annual Deb Star Ball held at the Hollywood Palladium. The event was covered by television, and a striking-looking Raquel was introduced along with nine other

An early publicity still for *A House Is Not A Home* with Raquel already unmistakable on the right

young girls as 'Ten Stars of Tomorrow'. Interestingly, of the ten girls – Wendy Washburn, Barbara Parkins, Beverly Stuart, Mary Ann Mobley, Laurie Sibbald, Margaret Mason, Donna Loren, Tracy McHale, Janet Landgard and Raquel Welch – only Barbara Parkins (in *Peyton Place*) and Raquel were destined for international stardom.

The year 1964, then, ended on a note of optimism: the first Raquel had enjoyed for some time. And the very next year saw the start of her dizzy rise to fame – and all because of a chance meeting in a coffee shop with a young, optimistic, though as yet unsuccessful publicity man named Patrick Curtis. It was at that moment – as more than one journalist and headline writer put it – that 'Svengali' walked into the life of Raquel Welch.

Raquel puts this crucial moment of her life into much simpler, less sensational and more objective terms: 'About nine months after I came to Hollywood, I met Patrick. I didn't know anybody else. He was only an office boy at Rogers & Cowan, a public relations firm. He quit to be my manager. A lot of wiseacres say our association was only "Business at first sight". But he was nobody, and I was nobody and we had very little weight to throw around. But we *did* have a very lovely romance.

'So we lived together and were inseparable for five years before we did marry. For the sake of my children, I tried to keep our real relationship hidden because I didn't want to be thought a scarlet woman. He became the real father to my children. He diapered and bottled my daughter Tahnee, who hadn't seen her real father since she was six months old.'

Despite his youthful looks, Patrick Curtis was fully conversant with the ways of Hollywood, having actually made his first screen appearance when still a baby. Born plain Patrick Smith, in 1937, he was just two years old when he won the Adhore Milk Company's Adhoreable Baby Contest which subsequently secured him the part of Olivia de Havilland's infant in the famous movie, *Gone With The Wind*. Next came a stint playing the ninth kid of the famous screen couple, *Ma and Pa Kettle*, and then six years until he was in his teens cast as Buzz in the TV series, *Leave It To Beaver*. Along the way he also changed his surname to Curtis out of admiration for his favourite film star, Tony Curtis. As a teenager, too, he began to get ideas about producing films rather than acting in them, and earned himself a master's degree in cinematography from USC by producing a documentary film about weightlifting. He was really just marking time at Rogers & Cowan waiting for the right opportunity to come along and developing what his friends have called a sixth sense for publicity, when he met Raquel.

Patrick was just twenty-eight and sensed *this* might be his moment, as he revealed to *Look* magazine in 1967: 'In Hollywood then, girls looked more like Sandra Dee than Sophia Loren,' he said. 'I was flabbergasted when this knockout told me she was a recent college scholarship student from San Diego – straight As, too. We decided to form an alliance and try to make her a star. I quit my job and we started a corporation we called Curtwel – something like opening a filling station – an honest business venture, with honest aims from the start.'

Time magazine saw the meeting in a rather more cynical light. 'Destiny's child and Beaver's buddy met in 1964 – smack in the poetic middle of Sunset Strip,' the publication alleged in November 1969. 'It was business at first sight. As Raquel recalls it: ''He saw me and I saw him and we put our heads together.''

Subsequently she reacted vehemently to this charge, telling *Rolling Stone* magazine in August 1974: 'That's really the lowest. Why do they think professional women are such barracudas? You're not going to pick somebody just to be a Svengali. Come *on*. If somebody loves you, it makes you feel like a million bucks. That goes for me and for the lady doing it under the fence with the man next door. She's gonna feel better.'

Patrick Curtis got to work promoting his 'discovery' right away. He arranged for her to have dancing lessons three times a week and singing lessons twice a week. He also utilised the knowledge he had gained at Rogers & Cowan for generating publicity by making her ever available to photographers. Whether stylishly but revealingly clothed on tennis courts or baseball parks, or else bikini-clad beside swimming pools or on the Hollywood beaches, she became a photographer's darling, and her instantly recognisable features were soon being spread lavishly throughout the pages of newspapers and magazines.

But Raquel was not about to let herself fall into the obvious trap of becoming just another dumb pin-up. She had shown her intelligence before and she would show it again. Although the photographs of her *appeared* to be casual, spur-of-the-moment snaps, in fact all had been carefully conceived. As Raquel herself explained years later, 'I had to know the occasion, the atmosphere, the reason. What I should wear, how I should do my hair, what I should be prepared to talk about.' These criteria have stood her in good stead from that day to this.

The appearance of her pictures in some of the better quality magazines – *Life* among them – began to get her noticed in film circles, and then her fourth film, undistinguished though it was once again, at least had her in a starring role.

The picture was *A Swingin' Summer*, in which she had fourth billing along with a number of luminaries including William Wellman Jr, the son of the famous film director, Maureen O'Hara's daughter, Quinn O'Hara, Garry Lewis, the son of comedian Jerry Lewis, and Allan Jones, father of the singer Jack Jones. The thin plot about a group of youngsters (including Raquel as Jeri) tracking down a group of hoodlums who have stolen the takings from a dance hall, could, as she herself later said, 'have been written on the back of a Band-aid'. The main purpose of the Robert Sparr directed movie was, in fact, to showcase several of the popular rock'n'roll groups of the time, including The Righteous Brothers, The Rip Chords and Gary Lewis and the Playboys. The highlights, such as they were, consisted of a race on water skis across Lake Arrowhead where much of the movie had been shot, and a motorboat chase ending in a happy pairing-off of the leading characters. Made by the independent company, United Screen World, *A Swingin' Summer* did at least have the distinction of giving rise to a record album of the soundtrack on which Raquel made her singing debut. It was to prove in this respect – if no other – a foretaste of things to come.

It was perhaps inevitable that all the exposure which Raquel was now getting as a result of her pin-up pictures would sooner or later catch the eye of a studio executive looking for new faces. And indeed that was just what happened. A batch of her pictures

Raquel, in her famous mini-dress, with Patrick Curtis at their wedding in Paris in 1967 was seen by producer Saul David at Twentieth Century-Fox. He did a double-take at the winning smile and spectacular figure and remembered that he had also seen this same girl the previous year at the Deb Star Ball.

Saul called up Patrick Curtis and had Raquel come over to Fox studios to make a test. He thought, initially, that she might make excellent decoration for a spy spoof he was in the process of setting up called *Our Man Flint*, starring James Coburn. However, as Saul David watched Raquel, and later talked to her, he had second thoughts. He decided to offer her a more substantial role in a Science Fantasy film called *Fantastic Voyage* which was also about to go into production at the Fox studios.

Raquel and Patrick – the embryo Curtwel – were delighted with this break. And also pleased at the chance of being associated with Fox which was now enjoying something of a revival in its fortunes after the costly *débâcle* of *Cleopatra* in 1962. Although Raquel did not yet see herself as a Sex Queen, Twentieth Century-Fox were the studio which had built an unknown girl named Marilyn Monroe into one of the world's greatest screen attractions, and under the guiding hand of Darryl F. Zanuck was busy making box-office winners again like the current hit, *The Longest Day*. Consequently, Raquel went into *Fantastic Voyage* full of optimism.

Right from the start, Saul David had decided that the picture was to be a *tour de force* of spectacular sets and special effects, and when the final cost of $6.5 million was computed, it all added up to what was then the most expensive science fiction spectacle of all time. This proved a good publicity line for the movie – and Raquel herself also got an enviable build-up in these releases when it was said she had 'won the role of scientist Cora Peterson over thirty "name" stars' – although no other names were actually disclosed.

The ingenious storyline by Otto Klement and Jay Lewis Bixby was set in the year 1995 when science had discovered how to reduce people and objects to the size of bacteria for short periods of time. When a defecting Czech scientist is shot in the head and put into a coma before he can reveal vital secrets about how to prolong this process, an extraordinary plan is devised to send a special miniaturised medical team into his bloodstream to operate on a clot in the middle of his brain and thus revive him.

The special effects transported Raquel and her co-stars, Stephen Boyd, Arthur Kennedy and the sinister Donald Pleasence, in a miniature submarine through a wonderworld of pink and white corpuscles the size of houses, into a whirlpool in the main artery, and then mistakenly towards a wildly pounding heart which threatens to smash their tiny craft to smithereens. After some breathtaking narrow escapes from the body's natural de-fence systems, the medics finally reach the scientist's brain where Donald Pleasence reveals himself to be an enemy agent and comes within a heartbeat of sabotaging the whole operation. In an equally clever finale, the successful team make their exit from the body along a tear duct and are rescued from a teardrop which looks the size of a small lake.

Director Richard Fleischer gave the picture the same sense of style and energy that made his earlier *20,000 Leagues Under The Sea* such a success, and not surprisingly the special effects later won an Oscar. The critics, however, were mixed in their opinions, although *Time* magazine in a pre-release review in August 1966 thought the picture might prove to be 'the most entertaining since the world was terrorised by a hairy rubber doll named King Kong.'

In Britain, when the film opened in September 1966, Felix Barker of the *Evening News* declared that *Fantastic Voyage* was 'an idea so preposterous that I believed every minute of it', while Alexander Walker of the *Evening Standard* wrote, 'Operation definitely a success', although he deplored the fact that no one made it clear whether the patient actually survived his ordeal or not. Judith Crist of the American TV programme, *Today Show*, was less impressed, telling her audience, 'It is a pity that the intellectual content never rises above Raquel Welch's bustline or Stephen Boyd's histrionic talents.'

There can certainly be no denying that Raquel was not well served by some of her dialogue. Most of the critics had fun at her expense over a line she delivered soon after the submarine had entered the scientist's bloodstream. 'Oxygenation!' she says. 'I never thought it would be like this!' And there was unintentional humour in another line she had to deliver to a leering Stephen Boyd, 'I run the laser beam here. That should tell you where to keep your hands.' Felix Barker in his review thought the film might also have been subtitled, 'With Raquel Welch Along the Jugular Vein'.

What no one could dispute, however, was that Raquel had caught the eyes of the cinema-going public. Despite the fact that she spent much of the picture inside the rubberised suit, this could not hide her figure, and she also gained most of the attention as the only female in the picture. A favourite moment among both critics and public alike was her dramatic fight with some tentacular antibodies which attacked her as if she were bacteria. Even Twentieth Century-Fox were pleased when the picture went on to make a highly creditable $5.5 million at the box-office.

Producer Saul David promptly rewarded Raquel with a non-exclusive contract at Fox, which unlike the Hollywood contracts of the past enabled her to work unhindered for any other film company as well as in television. Raquel was to become rather disparaging of her part in *Fantastic Voyage*: 'Although Twentieth Century-Fox billed me as a sex symbol in the picture,' she was to tell *Time* magazine in 1969, 'I was nothing but a rotten little nurse!' But she had achieved a breakthrough. It was her first picture of importance.

And when critic Tom Ferrell later summed up her achievement, he was pinpointing where her future now lay in a really uncannily accurate way: 'In *Fantastic Voyage* Raquel is reduced to microscopic dimensions and injected within the body of a sick man, where she assists in restoring the sufferer to health, a patent allegory of the goddess entering the life stream of mankind, working from within to restore and affirm the vital impulses themselves.'

But it was not into the far future that Raquel was destined to go to find real fame. Nor was she required to travel through the back-lots of Hollywood, but instead to cross the Atlantic and there confront the whole new film world of Europe . . .

Even managing to look sexy in a diver's suit in *Fantastic Voyage* (1966)

3 The Years of Cleavage

RAQUEL'S EMERGENCE AS an international celebrity was as sudden as it was dramatic. Following her debut in *Fantastic Voyage*, the Fox executives had planned a carefully managed campaign to establish her. 'We thought we would build her up slowly,' recalled Fox talent director, Owen McLean, in 1969. 'We thought it would take some time to make an impact. But she got more publicity by accident than most girls get on purpose.'

Once again, it was a chance meeting that was to bring Raquel a step closer to her dream. While she was waiting for *Fantastic Voyage* to be released, and feeling unsure as to when – or indeed whether – Fox might use her again, she met Ed Feldman, now an executive at Warner Bros, who often liaised between American and European film companies.

He was looking for a girl for the British film company, Hammer Pictures. Hammer had established a reputation for making horror films with such box-office successes as *Dracula* and *Frankenstein*, both featuring the accomplished actors Peter Cushing and Christopher Lee. But now they wanted to widen their range, and had completed a lavish production of the Rider Haggard classic, *She*, starring the sultry Ursula Andress and handsome John Richardson. They planned to use the same pair next in another old favourite, *One Million Years BC* which had previously been filmed in 1940 by Hal Roach and made a household name of a starlet called Carole Landis. History was all set to repeat itself when Ursula Andress, who was earmarked for the leading female role of Loana, turned it down.

Ed Feldman was impressed with the statuesque pictures he was shown of Raquel, and promptly mailed off a batch of them to Hammer in London suggesting that she might be just the girl they were looking for to play opposite John Richardson. As Fox released Hammer Pictures in America, they would be quite agreeable to loan her to their associates. Back came the word from London that Hammer would be very happy to take Raquel for this, their 100th movie. Immediately she and Patrick packed their bags. For Raquel, it was to be her first journey outside America.

The filming of *One Million Years BC*, the story of the love affair between Tumak and Loana, a Stone Age man and woman

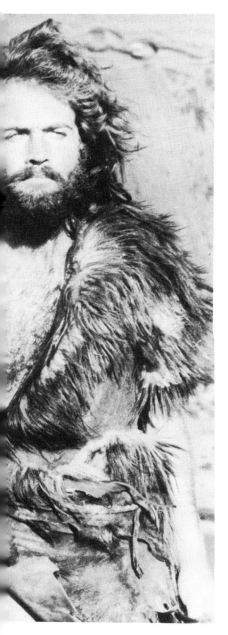

from warring tribes, was filmed partly on the Canary Islands and partly in London. Again a feature of the film was to be the special effects in the form of huge primeval monsters created by the master of film animation, Ray Harryhausen.

Raquel, though, had reservations about doing the film, having realised that it was her physical attributes that had landed her the part rather than any acting ability she might possess. Talking about this 'exploitation' to English film critic Victor Davis in 1969, she said: 'I'm not apologising. I was not brought up on the New York stage or in your National Theatre. I had to begin as an actress as best I could. Because of the instant fame, I have had to make my mistakes in public.

'There are so many selfish and egotistical reasons for becoming one, but once you are an actress you don't want to be thought of as a freak or a joke. You need to find out what uniqueness, what special flavour, only you can add to a role.'

So she gritted her teeth and got on with the film which was being produced by Michael Carreras and directed by Don Chaffey. She comforted herself with the thought, 'I was sure nobody would ever hear of the movie again. I could sweep it under the carpet and meanwhile get a trip to Europe. I thought, "Steve McQueen started by making *The Blob* and it didn't hurt him."'

However, her memory of working on *One Million Years BC* remains vivid, as she revealed when talking to Timothy Ferris in 1974: 'We filmed in the Canary Islands on the side of this volcano, and one of the first days I went up to the director and said, "I've been thinking about this scene and I think . . ."

'The director said, "You've got to be kidding. You've been *thinking* about this scene? See that rock over there? You just start from that rock and run across to that other rock, and that's all we want from you today."

'I said, "Well, don't you think that the girl, now that she's fallen in love with Tumak . . ."

'He said, "Listen, if you want something to do, there's going to be a giant turtle coming over that mountain, and when you get in the middle of the two rocks you can go 'Oh!' and do a take like you're frightened."

'I realised then that it really was a bad monster movie I was in, no way out of it. I had sold my soul to get to the Canary Islands.'

Although it is true Raquel had only three words to repeat in the film – *Akita* ('Help!'), *Seron* ('Giant pterodactyl') and *Tumak* (John Richardson's name) – her appearance was sensational and her costume ('Raquel Welch wears mankind's first bikini' was how it was later advertised) was to prove the starting point of her legend. If they gave her nothing to say, Raquel decided, then she would give *them* something to look at.

She was clothed, if such is the right word, in a chamois-leather loincloth and top. 'Between takes,' she says, 'I took out some scissors, snipped away at the costume, and just kept on snipping. It was also shrinking because of the continual soaking in the sea. There wasn't much to begin with, and I really had to watch it to keep it on at all.'

From such simple actions are moments of film history made. The bikini caught the eyes of the world's press and one journalist was to describe it as 'hardly big enough to wipe a car wind-screen'.

Patrick Curtis who had been keeping himself in the background until this moment, now sensed the time had arrived to promote Raquel for all she was worth. He obtained some photographs taken by a stills cameraman of Raquel in her stunning costume and commenced what turned into a remarkable and sustained publicity campaign.

First, he announced that Raquel Welch was Hollywood's answer to Ursula Andress, hoping to profit by the other actress's refusal to take the part of Loana. Secondly, he began to bombard newspapers and magazines with the now famous pose of Raquel in her ragged and revealing cave-woman outfit. It was an instant success with editors, and not long after came a huge-selling poster which found its way onto the walls of factories and offices all over the world. As *The News of the World* was to remark years afterwards, 'It (the photograph) was transmitted round the world – a spread-eagled picture of a blonde Raquel in taut animal skins, giving a global news value to a name few people knew and a picture fewer knew was being made. "The release of

Previous page: Raquel on location in the Canary Islands with John Richardson filming *One Million Years BC* and *(above)* a typical studio publicity picture for the movie

that one photo of me did it all,'' Raquel admits. And she is undoubtedly correct. ''And in this business when things like that happen you have to grasp it for all its worth.'''

Raquel spoke in somewhat more detail about this incredible moment in her life when she talked to *Penthouse* magazine in 1972: 'It was like a tidal wave that swept both Patrick and I away,' she said. 'Everything in our lives and careers changed almost overnight after *One Million Years BC*. Suddenly – after they had seen an unposed still photograph of me in rehearsal that later became *the* Raquel Welch poster – the world's press decided I filled a vacuum of being the ''New Girl Hot Number of The Moment''. All this has never quite died down. Now I realise I was really a little too grateful for this opportunity and the attention it brought me. I was nobody, and everybody impressed on me what a grand favour they were doing me by taking my picture and interviewing me. I tried to live up to what they thought I should be. I became a human dynamo-zombie working right around the clock. Patrick tried to prevent me from being exploited too much and he kept the children out of sight. I was glad that I had somebody to go home to and be with without putting on a show.'

Even while this 'tidal wave' was beginning to build up, Patrick was not wasting a minute. He and Raquel set out to tour Europe and capitalise on her newly-acquired fame. In the months which followed – the 'years of cleavage and personal appearances' as critic Byron Rogers has called them – Raquel seemed always in the eye of someone's camera, not to mention in the newspaper columns.

An early success occurred in March when she flew to London to attend the Twentieth Annual Royal Film Performance at the Odeon Theatre, Leicester Square, which premiered Carl Foreman's picture *Born Free*. Raquel not only met the Queen, but also stole the limelight and the newspaper headlines from the other stars who were present, including Ursula Andress whom she had replaced in *One Million Years BC*.

MEMORABLE MOMENT FOR RAQUEL WELCH – *The Daily Express* headlined its piece about the Film Performance on 15 March, with a large photograph of a stylishly dressed and obviously nervous Raquel shaking hands with the smiling Queen. The little girl from La Jolla had already come a long way, as another newspaper, *The News of the World,* was not slow to pick up: 'She was flown to London with all the fanfare accorded one just returned from a space flight . . . Raquel upstaged Ursula Andress in the reception line and all the photographers caught the Queen extending her hand to the unknown ''actress''.'

Raquel loved the film which was adapted from a best-selling true life story by Joy Adamson about an African lioness and the two game wardens who befriend her (played by Bill Travers and Virginia McKenna), but it was also an object lesson in what the future held. 'Even then things were starting to get out of hand,' she confessed two years later. 'When I met the Queen at the Royal Film Performance it was my picture that all the papers used, despite the fact that I'd gone out of my way not to wear a revealing dress.'

But there could be no doubting as the summer progressed, that Patrick Curtis' scheme was working superbly, and with each passing month Raquel became more a centre of attention wherever she went. Her willingness to pose made her very popular with journalists who soon came to appreciate that photographs of her stunning figure just about guaranteed publication of any story they might write. And by August 1966

Raquel meets Queen Elizabeth and steals the headlines at the Royal Film Performance in London in March 1966

she had run up the astonishing total of ninety-two front cover appearances in European magazines: no mean achievement for an actress so far without an internationally released film to her name.

The cost of all this – according to Curtis – was four badly damaged Cadillac limousines caused by the attentions of certain photographers who became just a little *too* persistent in their search for a really outrageous shot. And in Rome Raquel even had to 'arm' herself against intimate intrusions, as *Time* magazine reported in its issue of 24 June: 'Not so long ago in Rome, a stroller stopped at a traffic light and stared at the girl in the convertible. Was that a very short skirt she was wearing – or a long sweater? No matter; he couldn't stop looking. That was when the girl reached into her glove compartment, pulled out a pistol and let the gawker have it right between the eyes. It was only a water pistol, but it made its point. Raquel Welch doesn't mind stares, but she likes to choose the time and place. The time is now, but the place is pictures – the kind that move and the kind that stand still and stare back. Only last week she was simultaneously on the covers of no fewer than eight European magazines. The German *Quick* has put her on its cover nine times since January, and the French *Lui* recently ran fourteen pages of her photos, and hailed her "old-fashioned, hot, sensual return to the curve".

'There is only one flaw in Raquel's career so far,' *Time* added, 'No one has seen her movies.'

This point was not lost on Patrick Curtis who knew that pin-ups and magazine covers were all very well – but if Raquel was going to make it as an actress she needed to get more work in front of *movie* cameras. So, in quick succession and armed with the persuasion that Raquel's massive appearances in the media undoubtedly provided, he got her parts in no less than four European movies. The schedule was a punishing one, but invaluable for the experience it would provide. That Raquel *was* learning from her work was made evident by this quote she gave the press during her European soirée: 'In the studio you don't have an audience. But I don't miss them because I have my own. What I work for is the gratification of the director and cameramen, the men of quality. They are my real audience. If my director isn't satisfied, I can tell. Something comes off him and reaches you, just like an audience. Some actresses don't go to rushes. I always go. I always feel I have plenty to learn. What I am always looking for is that inner feeling that I have done right.'

Patrick added his comment, 'We feel that in choosing the right directors and veteran actors to work with her, she can learn more than in any other way. And, as you can see, she learns fast.' Almost as an aside, he told the journalists, 'Raquel's tragedy now is her lack of time to do anything *but* work!'

The first of this quartet of films co-starred her with a couple of real cinema veterans – the Italian, Vittorio de Sica and the American, Edward G. Robinson, who played two ageing gangster's in MGM's international co-production *The Biggest Bundle of Them All*. Youth came in the form of two fellow Americans, Robert Wagner and Godfrey Cambridge, as penniless young men in Naples who inveigle the old mobsters into joining forces to steal five million dollars' worth of platinum from a fast-moving train. Raquel is Robert Wagner's girlfriend, Juliana, who joins in the often farcical caper which almost succeeds until Wagner, flying the getaway plane, accidentally jettisons the hoard of hard-won ingots right into the path of the pursuing police.

Although the film did only modest business when it was released in 1968, Raquel's part as the capricious girlfriend came in for some notice by the critics. But it was her wild rock'n'roll dance with Edward G. Robinson that proved the highlight of her performance and got her dubbed as a 'delicious eyeful' by one writer.

Raquel stayed in Rome to make her second picture, *Le Fate*, another joint-production between Columbia Pictures and the Italian Documento Films. (This movie enjoyed a variety of bizarre titles when it was released in March 1968, including the most generally used, *Sex Quartet*, also *The Fairies*, *Les Ogresses* in France, and, in America, *The Queens!*) Billed as being 'in the tradition of Italy's boldest and most outspoken comedies', the film was described as 'exploring the erotic impulses of four beautiful women in search of sex'. Divided into four segments, the picture starred Capucine as 'Queen Marta' – a wealthy but haughty woman who seduces her manservant (Alberto Sordi); Monica Vitti as 'Queen Sabina' – a passionate, mini-skirted young woman who has to overcome the seeming indifference to her charms of Enrico Maria Salerno; Claudia Cardinale as 'Queen Armenia' – a beautiful, wild gypsy who falls in love with a sedate doctor (Gaston Moschin) and, finally, Raquel as 'Queen Elena'.

Raquel plays Elena the beautiful wife of a businessman who, while her husband is asleep in the garden, seduces a handsome neighbour (Jean Sorel) who arrives unexpectedly on a business call. Afterwards, it is the man who is racked with guilt about his indiscretion with the episode turning on its head the old saying 'A woman always pays'.

Time magazine, in what was to become almost a relentless series of bad reviews of her pictures, said of Raquel's performance: 'Weakest of the four queens is Raquel Welch (dubbed from American into Italian), whose story fortunately depends on the one thing she does best – registering no emotion.' By contrast, Alexander Walker of the London *Evening Standard* wrote, '*Sex Quartet* is much better than it sounds. It is four elegant, very smooth stories. Each tale is elegantly, effortlessly directed and acted with aphrodisiac sparkle by Monica Vitti, Claudia Cardinale, Raquel Welch and Capucine respectively.' And Felix Barker, of the *Evening News*, calling it a 'silky Italian portmanteau film', added: 'Just to get Monica Vitti (hitchhiking in a plunge-dress), Claudia Cardinale (doctor-seducing in a plunge-line dress) and Raquel Welch (husband-stealing in a plunge-back dress) is riches enough.'

The third picture of Raquel's Italian quartet, with the unlikely title, *Shout Loud, Louder, I Don't Understand*, gave her her most substantial part to date and, apparently, her biggest fee. She earned $60,000 plus several weeks of overtime. It also provided her with her first opportunity to work with a superstar, the Italian Marcello Mastroianni. Produced by Joseph Levine, it was based on a play *Le Voci di Dentro* by Eduardo De Filippo, who also wrote the screenplay and directed.

The centre of attention in Rome in the summer of 1966

Shout Loud, Louder, I Don't Understand is a rather typically strange, surrealistic Italian comedy in which Raquel plays Tania Mottini – a beautiful, deceptively immoral girl who becomes involved with a daydreaming artist-turned-villain, Alberto Saporito (Mastroiànni) who delights in making explosions. Sadly, the explosive climax to the film was not matched at the box-office where it flopped on its release in 1967. Raquel did not fare well at the hands of the critics, either, and Arthur Knight of the American *Saturday Review* represented the consensus of opinion when he wrote: 'And Raquel Welch, who in the past years has made more magazine covers than movies, here reveals the probable reason. As Mastroianni's dream girl, she looks great, but in every scene she seems as improbable as her dubbed-in-Italian dialogue.'

The last of the quartet of back-to-back films was almost a return to the kind of part with which she had begun her career in *A House Is Not A Home* two years previously. This was *The Oldest Profession*, a story of six episodes tracing the history of prostitution from the days of the cavemen through to the present day and even on into the future. For her role as a tart in Vienna in the gay 1890s, Raquel was paid $100,000, yet another indication of how her stature was rising, while the actual filming took no longer than two intensive weeks in Berlin.

As Nini, she discovers that one of her clients (Martin Held) is a rich banker and decides that better than taking his money it would be more to her advantage to marry him and quit her

Raquel with her co-stars in *The Biggest Bundle of Them All* (1967) and *(right)* in her lively dance sequence with the veteran Edward G. Robinson, from the same picture

present lifestyle. Raquel gave a beguiling performance in making the hapless banker believe that she loves him for himself, and then getting him to propose.

Once again the film did not enjoy much success at the box-office, though the futuristic episode directed by the talented Jean-Luc Godard and Raquel's episode did catch the eye of reviewers. Patrick Gibbs of the *Daily Telegraph* wrote in October 1967: 'The stories take us from prehistoric time to Jean-Luc Godard who comes up with a sort of yellowprint for *Alphaville*, suggesting that in a science fiction future, love and sex will have been separated once and for all. It is (as usual) lovely to look at . . . Of the rest, Michael Pfleghar's episode about a banker whom a courtesan rejuvenates shows a Maupassant feeling for the short story form, and has the advantage of Raquel Welch.' It is interesting to note in the light of these remarks that when the picture opened in France, Raquel was actually billed *above* two of her French co-stars, Jeanne Moreau and Anna Karina.

It may seem incredible in hindsight, but all these pictures were complete even *before* the movie which had splashed her face and figure across the world's magazines was actually released! But it is a fact that it was not until just before Christmas 1966 that *One Million Years BC* was premiered in London. Patrick Curtis, with another beautifully timed piece of promotion, arranged for 3,000 Christmas cards, measuring eleven inches by thirteen, each with Raquel's now famous cave-girl bikini shot on the front, to be sent to 'anybody who was anybody in the film business'. That stunning pose not surprisingly got pride of place over the traditional jolly Santa Claus and snowbound scenes on many a movie executive's desk that December!

Because of the enormous exposure which she had already enjoyed, it was only to be expected that the London critics would direct their attention to Raquel at the premiere on 21 December. John Russell Taylor, reviewer of that doyen of world newspapers, *The Times*, was clearly puzzled by the picture and not at all sure about its star:

'The only trouble, really,' he wrote, 'is the heroine Raquel Welch. She may, for all I know, be the greatest tragedienne since Duse, but she is lacking in the vital ability for this sort of

Raquel as Elena in *Sex Quartet* (1967) which was curiously retitled *The Queens* for release in America!

role, which is to scream and scream and scream again – what, otherwise, is the point of having a heroine set upon by a dinosaur or carried off by a pterodactyl? Now Carole Landis in the old version was not the greatest tragedienne since Old Mother Riley, but scream: that she really knew how to do . . .'

Cecil Wilson, of the *Daily Mail*, chose to lay on the adjectives even more thickly, though his comments only served to underline how well-known Raquel had now become: 'Sometimes that pneumatic American queen of premieres and magazine covers, Raquel Welch, actually makes a picture and this is one of those times. As a wild-haired beauty among the beasts, animal and human, in the savage dawn of history, an uncommonly well-set up member of the civilised Shell People at war with John Richardson's untamed Rock People, she liberally displays her legendary shape. She also fights like a tigress in what I take to be the first female all-in wrestling match – a ferocious contest of clawing, screaming and hair-tugging, waged against a mountain and desert background of the Canary Isles. Whether she can act, however, remains a moot point because all she is required to do apart from fighting is to run about a lot and say: ''Urgh!'', a word which almost exclusively serves the entire cast.'

An interesting feature about both these reviews – as well as several of the others – was that despite a fair amount of prejudice against Raquel, no one was prepared to state that she could not act. In fact there were even hints she might have a real talent, given the opportunity to display it.

Raquel, for this reason, has always had a special affection for London where, she says, she was 'more or less discovered'. Talking years later in 1974 she said, 'I've always credited, if it can be called credited, the British with discovering me when I made *One Million Years BC* for Hammer. At the time I thought it would be the kind of film that could be pushed under the carpet, but it rocketed me towards stardom. In fact, when I came back to Hollywood everyone thought I was English!'

Now that she was establishing herself as a personality – 'the girl who brought something of the old-style glamour back into the movies' as William Hall put it in 1970, adding: 'and also

A bit of fun for Raquel and her co-star Marcello Mastroianni at a press party for *Shout Loud, Louder, I Don't Understand*, while filming was going on in the summer of 1966

62

managed to become a global name before any of her films actually reached the public' – now that all this was happening, Patrick Curtis wanted to get the message across to the film community. In particular to the movie moguls back in Hollywood, the place which he knew Raquel would have to win over if she was ever to become a truly international star. That, he told himself, was his objective for 1967. That, and the little matter of some personal business between himself and Raquel . . .

A three-dimensional image of Raquel to promote *Shout Louder* – the first of its kind

4 The Sex Symbol of the Sixties

THE DUAL AMBITION of Raquel Welch and Patrick Curtis – for her to be accepted as more than just a tremendously successful pin-up – was given a very pleasant boost at the end of 1966 when the influential Hollywood trade newspaper, *Motion Picture Herald*, presented its annual list of 'Stars of Tomorrow'. For who should be there along with Elizabeth Hartman, Alan Arkin and Robert Redford, than – Raquel Welch.

Then, when *One Million Years BC* crossed the Atlantic and opened in America, several of the magazines and newspapers found themselves following the lead of their British counterparts to enthuse about its unpretentious objective of providing a colourful if fantastic entertainment. The *New York Times* was particularly keen on Raquel's performance, calling her 'a marvellous breathing monument to womankind'. And it added, perhaps more significantly, 'Nothing could look more alive and lasting than Miss Welch.'

Such comments could hardly fail to please Raquel, though she quickly went on record to stress that she wanted to be treated as more than just a pin-up who acted. 'I don't even try to be sexy,' she said. 'What I aim for is that kind of sensuality that foreign women – particularly Sophia Loren – have. That something which comes from inside.'

During the course of this hectic period which turned Raquel from a small-town girl trying to get a foothold in Hollywood to one of the most photographed women of the time, her relationship with Patrick had broadened and deepened, despite all the pressure they were under. Or perhaps, in hindsight, *because* of the pressures they were under. 'At the time I made *One Million Years BC*,' she said in 1968, 'a lot of people supposed me to be some kind of paper-doll, a mechanical contrivance manipulated by Patrick Curtis. It was understandable with the kind of publicity I was getting, I suppose. The people who saw me also didn't realise I had two babies at home in diapers at the time. Then there were those who tried to make something of that. I'd never made any secret about it – all my friends knew – it was just that I didn't choose to offer information about them at interviews. I think it is a bit unnatural to tell people you hardly know the details about your private life. Some actresses do it, I know, but I can't. We can hardly complain about being exploited in this business if we help to exploit ourselves.'

It seemed only natural, then, that having gone through so much, Raquel and Patrick should decide to get married. Two years earlier, in 1964, he had helped Raquel secure her divorce from James Welch, so there was nothing to stand in their way – if they could find the time. After the failure of her first marriage, Raquel did, though, have a few reservations, as she explained some years later in an interview given in 1972: 'Patrick and I decided to get married in early 1967. By then, we had been together five years, so it wasn't a marriage with the bliss of new love. For me, it was a consideration for my children, who thought of Patrick as their father. Patrick wanted it that way, too. Also, I had to please my family and I had an obligation to Patrick himself. Oh, I just don't know. If I had had a little more strength at the time, and hadn't been so tired and run-down, I might not have gone through with it. After the first time I was determined not to marry again. I still think I shouldn't have. But I would have been with Patrick anyway because I just don't believe in the nonsense of legality.'

The couple decided on a spring marriage in Paris – on St Valentine's Day, 14 February 1967. However, neither they, nor the authorities of the municipal building where the nuptials took place, had quite bargained for the pandemonium that ensued. As one of the most photographed women of the day, the press turned up in droves to see the knot tied.

Raquel remembers the event vividly – as if anyone who was either there, or read the reports afterwards, could possibly have forgotten it. 'When we got married in Paris it was absolute madness,' she says. 'People were dropping out of the trees to take photographs of us. For three days I had tried to get out to a couture house to buy a wedding dress, but I just couldn't because of the mob. In the end I wore a see-through crochet dress I'd bought at a London store. I thought: ''All right: you want something sensational – you'll get it.'' It was a rather miserable experience. You see, I couldn't understand why people were so interested. I hadn't behaved outrageously, or caused a scandal. Nothing. My private life was almost dull.'

As the daredevil sky-diver, Fathom Harvill, in *Fathom* (1967)

Miserable Raquel might have felt, but her appearance in that loosely-crocheted mini-dress sent the photographers 'into the kind of frenzy that piranha fish exhibit at feeding time', Byron Rogers reported afterwards. Nor was that quite the end of what became the most publicised wedding of the year – garnering hundreds of column inches of text and countless photographs – for in an anticipation of the famous bed-sit-in of John Lennon and Yoko Ono, Patrick and Raquel released pictures of themselves sitting up in bed together! (Film historian David Shipman has acidly called these photographs 'some sort of nadir in the annals of movie publicity'.)

The impact of all the attention that the press were giving Raquel finally had the desired effect on the executives back at Twentieth Century-Fox in Hollywood. Patrick Curtis had kept up a regular supply of cuttings to the studio and these, augmented by the coverage she was also getting from American newspapers and magazines, made Fox decide to exercise their option on her services and put her in one of their pictures.

So Raquel was offered the co-starring role with Tony Franciosa in a spy spoof entitled *Fathom* which was to be shot that spring in Spain. It meant she did not get to go home yet, but she decided to take it, anyhow. Although the picture was not the huge success everyone hoped, it gave the world another enduring image of Raquel, which is still remembered today almost as well as the cave-woman bikini. It was of her wearing a tiny, dazzling white bikini.

Raquel played Fathom Harvill, a member of an American sky-diving team who parachutes into a host of trouble at a Spanish aeronautics show. There she is recruited by a man claiming to be a member of NATO intelligence to help recover a nuclear device trigger mechanism which has apparently been lost in the Mediterranean. Two teams of foreign agents are also said to be after the same objective. It soon transpires that the man is not from NATO, nor are there enemy agents at work, but just an unscrupulous bunch of fortune hunters trying to use Fathom's skill in the air and underwater to recover a priceless figurine.

Work on the film proved hard and demanding, both on land

Another of Raquel's famous poses – in a soaked white bikini from *Fathom* (1967)

year had been worthwhile, here it was. The time had obviously been well spent in terms of experience gained and expertise learned. It also transpired in the fullness of time that the picture, which cost $1.8 million to make, eventually took $9 million at the box-office.

From the heat of Spain, Raquel flew to London for a cameo part in another Twentieth Century-Fox picture which was to prove her last in Europe before returning to Hollywood. The picture was *Bedazzled*, a reworking of the Faust legend produced and directed by Stanley Donen, in which Dudley Moore as a timid little cook in a hamburger restaurant sells his soul to the Devil (played as a kind of mod Mephistopheles by Peter Cook) in return for the favours of one of the waitresses, Eleanor Bron. It was the first full-length starring role for the comedy partnership who had become so successful on British television in *Beyond the Fringe*. (Dudley Moore, of course, has since become a Hollywood superstar, primarily as a result of his part with Bo Derek in *10*.)

In the *Bedazzled* script, written by Moore and Cook, the Devil grants the little cook seven wishes, which allows for seven excursions into satire as he courts the waitress firstly as a Welsh intellectual, then a cuckolded country house husband, a professor at Oxford, a millionaire, a pop star, a worldly-wise lover and, finally, and funniest of all, as a nun of the Order of Leaping Berelians.

Raquel made her appearance as 'Lillian Lust', one of the Seven Deadly Sins sent to harry the poor, bemused little cook. Although her time on screen amounted to only a few minutes, she displayed a skill for comedy which few people had suspected and which surprised every viewer of the film. One of the most memorable moments of the picture was her buffeting the distressed and innocent hero while clad only in a silver bikini. Thrusting out her breasts she demanded with evident mastery of the *double entendre*, 'Would you like hot toast – or buttered buns?'

Raquel was not only becoming more sure of herself when working, but when the studio was a happy one she also revealed a broad streak of humour in her nature. Fellow actors and technicians who worked on *Bedazzled* recall one particular example of this from her short time on the picture. During a break in the shooting, she and Dudley Moore went to relax in one of the dressing-room trailers. As the couple chatted, they became aware that some members of the crew were outside the trailer, eavesdropping. Giving a sly wink, Raquel suggested in a whisper to Dudley that they should pretend that they were making love. Accordingly – so the story goes – they went through the whole range of appropriate sound effects and emerged from the trailer to be greeted by a chorus of highly appreciative whistles!

The newspaper critics, too, appreciated *Bedazzled*, Alexander Walker and Ann Pacey particularly singling Raquel out for mention in their reviews in December 1967. Said Ann Pacey, 'Only Raquel Welch as Lillian Lust is a really effective deadly sin,' while Alexander Walker wrote: 'Raquel Welch incarnates the vice of Lust in a silver bikini and a body that suggests that she understudied for the part of the Serpent. The film may be just an extended series of variations on a revue sketch – but the fact is entertainingly concealed by the skill of all concerned.'

And when the film reached America the following March, *Playboy* concurred with the general opinion: 'Raquel Welch has seldom spoofed herself to better advantage.'

Having completed *Bedazzled*, Raquel and Patrick flew back to Hollywood to receive quite a welcome. American writers and journalists in their columns compared her rise to fame with that of Brigitte Bardot (who, incidentally, had also leapt to fame in Britain with her picture *Doctor At Sea*, made in 1955, after several undistinguished films in her native France), and were quick to quote Curtis when he said that Raquel had already appeared on the covers of over 500 magazines throughout the world! No one, he added, had even been able to *count* all the inside stories and ordinary newspaper photographs of her that had been published. She was truly the new sex symbol of the sixties, the reporters all agreed.

Speaking about her return to America, Raquel said in the following year, 1968: 'I never expected to get such a build-up. When I went back to Hollywood after getting all that publicity over in Europe, people said, ''You've been very clever, haven't you?'' They seemed to imagine that Patrick must have had some pull or known somebody. Of course, I realised I was being exploited and thought I could control the situation, but of course I couldn't. In the end I became quite paranoic about it. I felt I'd be such a disappointment to the people who'd read about me being a sex symbol that I almost stopped going out. I couldn't even go shopping without feeling self-conscious – waiting for the whispers: ''Is *that* all?'' – and feeling I was disappointing millions by just going shopping.'

Raquel's feelings about her 'sexploitation' caused her to turn down the next part she was offered by Twentieth Century-Fox – the first time she had taken such a course of action.

The part she was offered was one of the leading roles in *Valley of the Dolls*, based on the hottest-selling book of the time by Jacqueline Susann, which Fox had acquired against enormous competition from the other studios. They wanted her to play the part of Jennifer and shooting was due to go ahead almost immediately.

According to the head of the Fox Studios, Richard Zanuck, Raquel tested for the role, but then turned it down. 'It is unheard of for an actress to test for a role and then refuse the part,' he told journalists later. 'So I put her on suspension. Later on, though, I took her back.'

Raquel's reason for refusing the part was that she wanted to do other things than just play sexpots. 'If you have a physical attractiveness,' she said, 'you don't have to act. People don't expect anything of you. If they don't expect it, then it's not required to deliver it. But as an actress, I'd like to display the ability to act and I want the opportunity to do so.'

Film writer James Robert Parish has pointed out that this attitude becomes all the more understandable when one learns that at this time Raquel was becoming the new butt of endless jokes on television and in nightclubs, and didn't like it. Her figure was endlessly parodied, and she was often being referred to as 'the thinking man's Twiggy'.

Comparisons were also being drawn between her and Fox's sex goddess of a decade earlier, Marilyn Monroe – she was 'The Most Exciting Star Since Marilyn Monroe', a 'dark-haired

Monroe' it was said – which were equally stultifying, and Raquel responded to such claims by telling the ever-inquisitive journalists: 'I wouldn't like to be like her. I certainly don't envy her. She was very unhappy and took her life because she felt she was so inadequate. She felt nobody liked her except for physical appeal alone. That's very dangerous for a woman because you can't be young and beautiful forever.'

Almost as if she wished to exorcise the demons of such thoughts, Raquel went back to her origins and did some television work during the autumn of 1967. Indeed, she went right back to the show where she had begun as a Billboard Girl, ABC's *The Hollywood Palace* – though now she was a featured performer. A show with Sammy Davis Jr obtained some of the highest audience ratings of the season.

One delightful experience followed another when Bob Hope asked her to join him in his Christmas USO tour to Vietnam. Whatever reservations she might have felt about travelling to the war-torn country were instantly dispelled by the warmth of the welcome she got from the troops. She was undeniably the hit of the tour and sang, danced and performed for the servicemen with enormous charm and enthusiasm. On her way home, she told a journalist, 'Before Vietnam, I thought being me was a bum rap. Then the first day there they had these great big posters of me! I could see how much the tours meant to those boys and it was all just so worthwhile.' Raquel was also delighted when part of her act was featured in a Bob Hope Special about the Christmas Tour.

The New Year began with a flurry of activity once again. Two of the films she had made during her time in Europe, *The Biggest Bundle of Them All* and *Sex Quartet*, were released in America in January and March respectively to cash in on her vaulting popularity (in the States *Sex Quartet* was, of course, curiously retitled *The Queens*), while she was busy on a new project for Fox, her first Western, *Bandolero!* (Coincidentally, *Valley of the Dolls* had just been completed with the ill-fated Sharon Tate playing the part Raquel refused.)

Although the story of *Bandolero!* was set in Texas in the period immediately after the Civil War, much of the location

Raquel's delight and
exuberance while entertaining
US troops in Vietnam with
Bob Hope in December 1967 is
splendidly caught in these two
photographs

shooting took place in Page, Arizona as well as the sprawling, sagebrush country around Bracketville, Texas. Under the harsh sun and faced with a demanding role, Raquel experienced what location shooting far from civilisation can really be like.

Co-starring with her were the veteran Western actor, James Stewart, and the entertainer, Dean Martin, as two brothers who are reunited in Texas after fighting on opposite sides in the Civil War. Discouraged by the devastation they find in the aftermath of war, both head for the booming state of Texas to carve out new lives the best way they can – by looting and killing. Stewart portrays a veteran of the Northern army which campaigned through Georgia under General Sherman, while Martin is a veteran of Quantril's Raiders and seems unable to forget the hard charging 'easy come, easy go' pattern of life that dominated the Southerner's guerilla operations.

Raquel played Maria Stoner, the wife of a Texas rancher who is killed by Martin. She is taken hostage by the two men who decide to use her to aid their escape from the pursuing posse led by another veteran Western actor, George Kennedy. Director Andrew V. McLaglen developed the relationship of the captive woman and her husband's murderer from violent hatred to simmering passion with a mixture of gritty realism and touches of nicely-played humour.

Shooting a section of the picture in Utah proved literally torturing when a sandstorm got up, erupting around the crew and actors. Martin and Stewart were at least protected by bandannas, but Raquel had nothing to prevent the sand lashing into her hair, eyes, nose and ears. 'That night I must have washed a ton of red sand out of my hair,' she said afterwards. 'And all day my eyes were watery.'

An even tougher moment came when the actors were filming a crossing of the Rio Grande at a place called Devil's River, Texas, about fifty miles north of Del Rio. The horse Raquel was riding suddenly stumbled on the hard rocky bottom and she was thrown out of the saddle. 'Fortunately I got my boots out of the stirrups as the horse fell,' she recalls, 'and I managed to get free enough so I wasn't harmed too much. But I did still get a badly bruised ankle and a scratched foot.' The injuries did not prevent

With Dean Martin filming *Bandolero!* (1968)

80

her from working, although she ended the picture with the marks to show that she had learned about location shooting the hard way!

Bandolero! was released in July 1968 and quickly proved a box-office success, making over $5.5 million. The critics were, though, more impressed by the carefully handled lack of morality in the film: an unusual departure for Westerns which usually painted all the characters in very definite shades of black or white. Raquel as the rancher's wife had been at the heart of this situation, and was complimented in a rather back-handed way by the critic of the *New York Post*: 'Raquel Welch, the nobly endowed, chaste lady, confesses in pseudo-Latin accents that she had been a slightly sordid citizen and that her late husband had bought her from her poor father for ''five cows and a gun''. All things considered, that's the best buy in *Bandolero!*'

From the hostile environment of Texas, Raquel's next assignment could not have provided a greater contrast: it took her to the millionaire's playground of Miami in Florida to film a private eye thriller with Frank Sinatra. The picture was *Lady In Cement*, a sequel to Sinatra's *Tony Rome* (1967) in which he had played a wise-cracking private detective who lives on a boat and takes on seemingly impossible assignments. Raquel was cast as Kit Forrest, a wealthy alcoholic who Tony Rome discovers has been framed for murder by a local mobster, and when he has proved her innocence, takes off with her to the Bahamas.

When the movie was released in November 1968, John Mahoney of *The Hollywood Reporter* was enthusiastic: '*Lady In Cement* follows in the gumshoe ruttings of *Tony Rome* but has the better fortune to follow Frank Sinatra's hit, *The Detective*. The sequel to Sinatra's original Miami Beach lounge act is better on several counts. It manages to have fun at its own expense rather than relying wholly on leering bad taste. While it continues Fox's recent breakthrough in nipple exposure and again drags on the fags, broads and hoods who people the world of small time private eye Tony Rome, the film has a fresher script, lighter hands playing, and the same sharp direction and cinematography.'

In London, *The Times* and the *Daily Sketch* also liked the picture and both gave approving nods to Raquel's performance and the moments of comedy she had been able to inject into her role. Said John Russell Taylor of *The Times*: 'Raquel Welch as a society drunk is, I think deliberately, a rather funny lady.' And the *Sketch* concurred: 'Raquel Welch gives a performance of some wit, still parading that mighty frame.'

Raquel herself, however, was not altogether happy with the picture, but did enjoy working with Frank Sinatra. 'He has the most raw talent and magnetism of any man I've met,' she said later. Raquel also took advantage of the fact that her co-star was singing in Miami in between filming, and went to see him. 'While we were filming, Frank was working at the Fontainebleau,' she said, 'and it was a revelation to see him in front of an audience. To completely hold people the way he did is a remarkable thing. I decided right there, "I'm going to keep that part of my talent alive".'

Although she had, of course, been singing and dancing since she was a child, it was at that moment, says Raquel, that she got the impulse to 'storm the supper-club stage'. It was to prove no idle threat, either, for in the years which followed she was to develop a nightclub act that could wow an audience in even such hard-bitten show business meccas as Las Vegas and New York, and would also prove the basis for some of her later television specials and, ultimately, her Broadway musical triumph.

But such things were still a long way off in 1968, although Raquel could look at her achievements so far with some degree of satisfaction. When she had first burst into the public eye she was usually referred to as 'The Girl Who Can Speak With Her Body', and there were those who seriously doubted whether she would ever be anything other than just a body. The proof that her talent went beyond such clichés was, though, by now convincing even such hard-bitten show business writers as Britain's Roderick Mann that she was a lady to be reckoned with. He wrote in his column of 30 June 1968: 'Time, happily, has proved Miss Welch to be loquacious as well as lovely limbed. What's more, a spot check of Instant Opinion, carried out in the pouring rain the other night, still had her romping home as the girl most people would like to be cast away with.'

In conversation with Roderick Mann, Raquel showed that she could be very objective about herself despite all the hysteria. 'I'm not particularly satisfied with myself physically,' she said. 'I don't think I'm the end-all whatever they say, though I know I have quite a nice figure. I've never considered myself a raver. I like looking at beautiful women, but I find it very difficult to have women friends. Pretty girls don't seem to want to be friends with me. Another thing, I find I influence other women quite a lot. If someone comes to work for me as a housekeeper, say, or secretary, within a short time I find them wearing the same sort of clothes and hairstyle. It's flattering, I suppose, but vaguely irritating.'

Raquel also had some pertinent remarks to make about men. She revealed herself to have little in common with the fervent women's libbers of the time. 'Men are changing,' she said. 'It used to be fun fighting for independence as a girl. Now there's no fight any more. Men have given in. I wish they hadn't. Most women feel the same way as I do, you know. They want men to behave in the classic way and dominate them. It's very unsettling for women to find themselves with men who aren't sure of their manhood. Unfortunately that type of man is on the increase!

'Some women too seem to have gone completely overboard. I've just been reading about SCUM (the Society for CuttingUp Men – a man-hating society in the US). Just reading about that kind of lunacy is horrifying.'

The interview with Roderick Mann demonstrated that Raquel was not afraid of controversy, nor was she afraid of taking a firm stand on issues that she felt strongly about. She could, though, have had little way of knowing that in the next stage of her career she was to be at the very centre of controversy on two crucial issues: nudity and pornography.

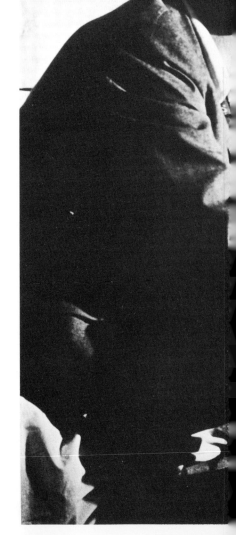

With Frank Sinatra in a tense
moment from their movie,
Lady In Cement (1968)

5 The Nudity Campaign

BY THE YEAR 1969 there were those in the film industry who were already beginning to regard Raquel Welch as almost a superstar. In a short space of time she had become an extremely bankable name at the box-office – whatever critics might feel about the films she had made – and the public were going to see her in increasing numbers, making for a very healthy return for the investors in her pictures. Indeed, a Reuters poll of worldwide film exhibitors at this time reported that Raquel was now among the top ten box-office draws. Once again, though, just as she had shown in her interview with Roderick Mann, Raquel could be extremely objective about the business of film-making.

'Everyone pays a lot of lip service to sensitivity and artistry,' she complained in April 1969. 'But when you come right down to it, it's all money and shooting schedules. They want to be able to write everything out like a financial statement and come out with a neat little sum at the bottom.'

She could also be equally objective when tested by journalists about claims that she was a superstar. 'Yes,' she agreed, 'superstars get to a point where they want to put themselves on a pedestal. Liz Taylor has always been flamboyant, though. Sophia Loren came up from nowhere and her stardom has meant social snobbery. Success for me doesn't mean social position. It means satisfaction and not being upset by the public's thinking of me as sensual. But right now, too many people when they meet me have a misconception about what I'm going to be, some sort of Amazon superwoman.'

What was beyond any dispute by this time was the hefty fee that she could command for a picture – according to *Time* magazine her contracts now called for $330,000 per film plus a percentage of the gross.

The joint partnership of Welch and Curtis – Curtwel – were of course only too well aware of Raquel's status at the box-office and not surprisingly began to give serious consideration to making their own movies. In December 1968 the couple announced that they had purchased the rights to a novel called *Tilda*, about a woman's pursuit of her kidnapped son, written by Elizabeth Kata, author of the Oscar-winning film, *A Patch of Blue*.

Just one extraordinary moment among many in *The Magic Christian* (1970)

The heroine in the stor   /as a Liverpool girl, which naturally enough brought the owr   s of Curtwel Productions to England at the turn of the year, ' find out what a Scouse accent sounded like. The accent posed o fear for her, Raquel told reporters, but she was considering ianging the setting to San Francisco for greater dramatic ir   act. For the part of her mother in the story she had thought (Ava Gardner, still very beautiful at forty-six years old. The r ject, she said, was one in which she hoped 'to find out what   am capable of. It isn't enough just to be doing what I have een doing,' she went on. 'I need a challenge to keep my s   respect. Oh, it was all right for the first few years. So muc^   as happening I didn't have time to think. But now I do, wh   i is why I intend to make films which don't just use me as d   ration. You get to the stage, you know, when you become si   f the fact that your physical presence distracts people from   iting to hear what you have to say; when they regard you   ercly as some sort of ornament. Oh sure, I'm grateful for what my looks have brought me, but now I want to do what I've wanted to do ever since I was five years old. And that is act. When Patrick and I formed our independent production company people thought I was being pretentious. But I'm determined to try to live down my initial image, however hard it proves. Most people get stuck with some kind of image early on – Marilyn as a dumb blonde, Karloff as a monster – and find it hard to live down. And this is a business of images, of course. Which is fine until that image begins to limit you, which is what's happening to me now. Anyway, in a business which boasts people like Paul Scofield and Maggie Smith, what pride can there be in just getting by on your looks and figure?' she added.

Unfortunately, other pressing commitments caused *Tilda* to go on the shelf. Raquel was required in Spain to work on a contracted picture for Fox, another Western, *100 Rifles*. It was to prove a film almost totally overshadowed by events off-camera rather than on.

Raquel was cast as Sarita, a Mexican Yaqui Indian who dedicates her life to avenging the murder of her father, killed by the ruthless military forces of General Verdugo (Fernando

Lamas). A half-breed, Yaqui Joe, played by Burt Reynolds, robs a bank to provide the Indians with rifles for their fight with the General, but the plan is complicated by the arrival of a black US deputy sheriff (Jim Brown) determined to arrest Yaqui Joe and return him north of the border where the robbery was committed.

Before work on the picture began, the partnership of Raquel and Jim Brown was heralded as a unique meeting in the Wild West of a 'lusty Othello and his lissom Desdemona'. Although Fox rightly suspected that the casting of a white woman and a coloured man would almost certainly get the film banned in cinemas in the Southern states of America, it was believed the picture would help in the demolishing of racial barriers – as well as making for good box-office. The fact that the couple ultimately fall in love during the course of *100 Rifles* added still further to the potential.

There was interest, too, in the fact that there was a curious parallel in the careers of Raquel and Jim Brown, a six foot two inch former professional footballer with the Cleveland Browns. He had made his debut at Fox in 1964 in *Rio Conchos*, the same year, of course, that Raquel was making *Roustabout* and *A House Is Not A Home*. Like her, too, his name soon became a guarantee at the box-office on any film regardless of quality, although his performance in *The Dirty Dozen* and *Ice Station Zebra* particularly justified his promotion to a super-charged sex symbol.

According to producer Marvin Schwartz, the part of the lawman had originally been written for a white man, but he became convinced that Brown's male magnetism would outweigh any considerations of colour. The director, Tom Gries, was also in no doubt about his intentions: 'I am encouraging them to act as a man and a woman,' he said, 'without any thought of holding back because the colour question might upset some people. We won't pull any punches. There is no courtship: she goes straight from antagonism to passion. She tells him: ''You are my man.'' And that settles the whole situation as far as she is concerned.'

According to show business writer Victor Davis, Raquel insisted on meeting Jim Brown before the filming began. 'She wanted to see if any chemistry existed between them,' he wrote. ' "I found Jim a warm, sensitive man," Raquel said.'

That indeed may well have been her view before work began but once on location the 'chemistry' went badly wrong. Mary Bredin, who met Raquel during the course of filming *100 Rifles* and later became her confidante, says that things between the couple were soured right from the outset when Brown greeted his co-star with, 'So you're the new sex symbol. Lady, have you got them fooled. My tom cat's got more appeal than you.'

The relationship deteriorated even further, according to *Time*, when racial overtones began to creep into off-camera remarks. 'Brown did little to smooth the situation,' said the magazine on 28 November 1969. 'At lunch he growled at her: "Pass the salt; it isn't black." She (Raquel) and Brown finally stopped talking altogether.'

Despite the hostility, the picture was completed, and afterwards, far from the scorching climate of Spain, Raquel was able to talk calmly about what had gone wrong. 'In some respects it was a very good experience for me,' she said. 'From now on I know I'll never find anyone difficult again. For nobody could possibly top that man. It was just awful. Right from the beginning I realised it wasn't going to work. The situation between us became so bad that I found myself apologising to him, although I'd done nothing. "Whatever I've done I'm sorry," I said. "I just want us to get along together." But it was no use.'

How, though, had she been able to shoot the love scenes which had been so crucial to the plot, Raquel was asked. Giving a wry smile, she replied, 'Listen, they shot the key love scene on our very first day together. Those rotten sons of bitches knew we wouldn't get along and wanted to make sure they had the love scenes wrapped up early.'

The making of *100 Rifles* also brought Raquel into confrontation with Twentieth Century-Fox on a matter about which she has very strong and inflexible views: screen nudity. A scene in the film called for her to strip. She had to distract a bunch of marauding soldiers with her naked body. It was not the kind of scene she had done before and she was not about to do it now.

The controversial 'nude' publicity shot for *100 Rifles* (1969) with co-star Jim Brown

Overleaf: Raquel with Burt Reynolds and Jim Brown in a dramatic moment from *100 Rifles*

To this day it remains an extraordinary fact that despite the impression so many people have that Raquel has been seen nude in magazines and on the screen, she has actually *never* appeared naked in public. For years, in fact, her contracts have contained a stipulation that she will not be called upon to appear undraped.

'I am proud of the fact I have never appeared in the nude,' she emphasises. 'It is a very personal thing to take off your clothes. I refused to do this nude scene in *100 Rifles* and for weeks the telegrams flew back and forth, arguing about who was going to get me to do it. I mean could you see me waving a rifle and bounding among a party of Mexican Indians starkers? They couldn't convince me that stripping off was either logical or reasonably motivated. Finally, they gave up. I played my scene with clothes on, but they had their nude scene as well. They brought in another little lady to take her clothes off. It's so depressing that commercial interests should always override aesthetic considerations.'

Raquel returned to the subject again when *100 Rifles* went on general release in April 1969. (She also replied to the cynics who pointed the finger of accusation at her bare-backed publicity photograph taken with Jim Brown, that there had actually been a towel between them when the picture was taken.) 'Nudity is now being taken for granted in films,' she said, 'and that's very dangerous. Personally, I think it's a bore. And, anyway, what is all this about nudity being sexy? Don't people ever think of teeth and lips and the backs of necks as being erogenous zones? For that's what they are to me.'

Victor Davis, who had written optimistically of Raquel's pairing with Jim Brown, was fascinated by her statement, and under a heading, 'You Will Never See Me Starkers says Raquel Welch', wrote in the *Daily Express* of 19 April: 'The campaign against explicit sex in the cinema gained a determined, not to mention surprising, recruit yesterday. "It's really getting to be *degrading*," said Miss Raquel Welch. Now you might think that Miss Welch, whose animal presence and awesome bodywork have launched a million magazine covers and a clutch of movies notable more for their box-office success than their artistic value, should be the last person to talk. Yet the lovely creature was quite vehement. "You've never seen me wearing anything less than any girl would wear on the beach," she said. "I saw a lesbian scene in *The Killing of Sister George* and thought it the most degrading, horrible thing. I could never do anything like that. What we are seeing now in many films is just blatant pornography. It never ceases to amaze me the limits to which actresses can go. They must be desperate for attention." '

Raquel's achievement of reaching the pinnacle of her profession without ever appearing naked is an astonishing one that deserves examination when you consider – as *Time* magazine wrote in November 1969 – that nowadays 'sex has been stripped of its last, diaphanous shred of symbolism'. How could someone like her succeed against such odds, the publication asked, attempting the tricky job of explaining her appeal.

'This is the Age of Lubricity,' it began, 'a time of topless shoe-shine parlours and bottomless go-go dancers, of mouthwash ads that assure sexual triumph, of the Pill and unlimited campus overnights. Films like *I Am Curious (Yellow)* and *Coming Apart* depict explicit sexuality at your friendly neighbourhood theatre. Yet somehow there is still Raquel the Sex Goddess, who has bared neither entire breast nor buttock to the public eye, and whose career has never been galvanised by the iridescent zinc of scandal. Even she admits: "I think that the whole sex symbol thing is an anachronism".'

The essence of her appeal, the magazine believed, 'lies beyond the relatively civilised pale of the Frantic Forties, or even the Salacious Sixties. Whether squaring off in well-cleaved wolf-skin against grumpy pterodactyls (*One Million Years BC*) or driving the *federales* from the Yaqui Indians' charnelled fastness (*100 Rifles*), Raquel is raw, unconquerable, antidiluvian woman. She dwells on the dark side of every man's Mittyesque moon; she is the nubile savage crying out to be bashed on the skull and dragged to some lair by her wild auburn hair.

'At the same time, Raquel's atavism has the advantage of posing no threat to uncertain, post-Freudian man. Modern Man may indeed be no match for Wonder Woman, but his masculinity is not imperilled by such barbaric, unreal imagery. Today's male moviegoer can gambol with Raquel in fantasies

Raquel's relationship with Jim Brown was stormy both on the set of *100 Rifles* as well as off it

95

and still not be discomforted by the possibility – in conscious, relatable experience – of ever having to do anything about it. This curious sense of inaccessibility distinguishes Raquel from a forerunner such as Bardot, who always seemed on the verge of sashaying off the screen and seducing the curly-haired kid in the second row. Producers have been careful to preserve and exploit this cinematic paradox; it is surely no accident that Raquel rarely plays an ordinary human being, much less an authentic romantic object.'

Though *Time* magazine might not have entirely succeeded in its explanation, it had at least placed on record a unique feat – and one from which Raquel has never deviated. Nor ever seems likely to.

Though the problems of making *100 Rifles* had certainly given Raquel a platform on which to expound her viewpoint on nudity in the cinema, she could not disguise her disappointment with the film – a verdict perhaps coloured by all the trouble.

'Oh, listen,' she told the press later. 'I know I'll probably never be satisfied. But after I'd seen *100 Rifles* I didn't come out of my gloom for a week. I thought it was the worst movie ever made and my performance the worst ever given.'

This was not, however, a view shared by some of the film critics. *Showguide Monthly*'s reporter waxed positively lyrical: 'As Sarita, Miss Welch is a revelation . . . improving even on her good work in *Bandolero!* Sarita is a guerilla fighter; all woman, all spitfire, using her body as a weapon every bit as effectively as her rifle. "She's not my favourite gal," Raquel told us. She's a vast improvement on Raquel's bikini-modelling roles, however.'

In America, Judith Crist in *New York* magazine, reported: 'Miss Welch, by the way, is not only the body beautiful in any colour, but emerges dramatically with Lynn Fontanne stature.'

Whatever anyone else might have thought, Fox laughed all the way to the bank, their takings more than trebling the cost of $6 million.

Before returning to America, Raquel stopped off in London once again, to play a cameo role in Commonwealth United Pictures' adaptation of Terry Southern's black humour novel, *The Magic Christian*. She was cast as 'The Priestess of the Whip', urging on a crew of eighty topless rowers – apparently the motive force of a new exclusive kind of luxury liner. Raquel shot her scene with co-star Ringo Starr at Twickenham Studios in a day, and barely had time to meet Peter Sellers, cast as the central character, an anarchistic billionaire called Sir Guy Grand, dedicated to inducing people through large sums of money to perform bizarre spectacles for himself and his adopted son (Ringo).

When the picture was premiered in December 1969, the initial high hopes of turning an underground classic novel into a brilliant, satirical film were dashed: most of the critics shared the view of Michael Billington of *The Times* that it was 'over-explicit and coarse-textured'. If there was anything to admire in this film which had been partly scripted by Terry Southern (who, of course, was also the author of the famous sex comedy novel, *Candy*), and director Joseph McGrath, then – said Ian Christie of the *Daily Express* – it was the practical jokes. And he wrote: 'The biggest practical joke of all is a fabulously expensive cruise for top people which turns out to be a nightmare, even though the ship is powered by numerous half-naked girls lashed into activity at their oars by voluptuous Raquel Welch.'

It was perhaps significant in the light of her now-established box-office appeal, that despite the presence of Sellers and the Beatle Ringo Starr in his first screen role, it was a photograph of Raquel, whip in hand, which was used extensively to publicise and promote the picture.

Once she was back in America, Raquel found herself shuttling backwards and forwards between Los Angeles and Las Vegas to play a nightclub dancer in MGM's *Flare-Up* which gave a vivid picture of the seamy side of the entertainment world. To star in this picture, Raquel picked up a salary in excess of $300,000 and offered audiences two memorable moments – firstly, performing a dance sequence at the Pussy Cat A-Go-Go Club in Las Vegas, and then driving her car in a breakneck chase sequence through the Griffith Park Zoo in Los Angeles.

Mark Rodger's story tells of the relentless pursuit of three beautiful go-go dancers (Raquel, Pat Delany and Sandra Giles) by a psychotic killer (Luke Askew) who believes that the mind of one of the girls – his estranged wife – has been poisoned against him by the other two. Director James Neilson kept up a relentless pace as first the wife and then one of her friends are picked off by the killer who then homes in on the terrified third girl, Raquel. No matter how she tries to avoid her pursuer, he is always just a step behind, his uncanny ability to anticipate her next move pushing her towards the brink of madness. To save herself Raquel has to hurl a can of gasoline over the killer and turn him into a human torch.

Once again the critics were generally hostile to the picture, although the public turned up in droves when it was released at the end of the year. Despite her undoubted popularity and continuing rise up the box-office charts, Raquel was growing increasingly tired of the unsubstantial parts she was being offered. And what's more the strain of her work schedule was frequently leaving her tired and depressed. In a confessional frame of mind she told Roderick Mann: 'You know I really don't think I could function if I weren't an actress. I feel I'm nobody when I'm not acting. Without a role to think about or look forward to, I can't tell you how depressed I get. But there is a price to be paid. I suffer very badly from tension headaches, sinus trouble and bouts of total fatigue. I am also allergic to something that makes my face puff up. I find it so difficult to relax. Patrick pulls on my head, sometimes, to relieve the tension. Other times I just roll my head around or chew some pills. They haven't been able to find out what I'm allergic to. It's a bit like being in a concentration camp and the doctor's trying to get information out of you that you simply haven't got.

'The other night I called my doctor and told him I couldn't sleep. "What are you taking?" he asked. "Two little red pills," I said. "Well," he said, helpfully, "try three." I did, and they put me out like a light. But it worries me you know. Three is rather a lot. I'm beginning to feel like one of those girls in *Valley of the Dolls.*'

It was perhaps curious that Raquel should have referred to the picture she had refused to appear in, but the message seemed to be loud and clear. She needed a really substantial part in a challenging picture. Something to demonstrate that she was more than just a very beautiful body: an actress of genuine talent and range.

In fact the opportunity lay just around the corner as she entered her thirtieth year. It was to come in one of the strangest and still most controversial pictures of the seventies – in which Raquel would find herself cast as a man playing a woman!

As a stunning go-go dancer in
Flare-Up (1969)

6 **Woman Into Man**

WHEN TWENTIETH CENTURY-FOX announced that they had bought the screen rights to arguably the most sensational bestselling novel of the decade, Gore Vidal's *Myra Breckinridge* – 'the book that was burned and banned on its way to the bestseller list' according to the *Daily Mirror* – the world was frankly astounded. Vidal's extraordinary, talented, cynical, notorious and often very funny book about a transvestite who sets out to conquer Hollywood and devastate mankind, seemed too outrageous for the screen, too savage a parody of Hollywood for anyone to risk adapting it. Yet the company fanfared their purchase of the book – which Vidal himself was to turn into a screenplay – and then gave rise to even bigger headlines when announcing that Raquel was to play the leading part of Myron-who-becomes-Myra. Some papers were amazed, others bemused, a few horrified – *The Times*, though, was later to call it 'a master stroke'.

Raquel herself was cautious in her first pre-filming statement to the press, realising only too well because of the story and the other actors who were being lined up to appear with her (Rex Reed, John Huston, Farrah Fawcett and the veteran Mae West) that the months ahead would be fraught with pitfalls. 'Look,' she said, 'it obviously isn't my dream part. But it's the first real role I've ever been offered. And it's the first time I'll be able to exercise myself as a comedienne. Image? I don't think one role, even this one, can hurt that. As a matter of fact, the whole campy, sex symbol thing has gone too far in one direction as far as I'm concerned. Playing Myra will probably do me more good than harm.'

Twentieth Century-Fox had apparently given a tremendous amount of thought to casting her in the lead, and among other names also considered – so the rumours said – were Elizabeth Taylor, Angela Lansbury and Ann Bancroft. Eight real transvestites had even been tested, but found unacceptable. The credit for picking Raquel went to producer Robert Fryer, a veteran of the Broadway stage and the man behind another controversial movie, *The Prime of Miss Jean Brodie*. He told the press how his inspiration came about: 'If a man were going to become a woman he would want to become the most beautiful woman in the world. He would become Raquel Welch.'

Raquel in *Myra Breckinridge*
(1970)

Aside from the potentially explosive cast, Fox decided on handing the direction to a twenty-nine-year-old English former pop star turned director, Mike Sarne. No stranger to headlines himself – he had rocketed to fame with his very first record, 'Come Outside' and then in 1966 landed a movie role co-starring with Brigitte Bardot in *Two Weeks in September* (and for a time was one of her lovers) – Sarne soon became embroiled in a situation that threatened to become even more explosive than the film itself.

Time magazine which reported the making of *Myra Breckinridge* in lurid step-by-step detail, wrote in November 1969: 'Not since *Cleopatra* has a movie provoked so much gossip, speculation, expectation – and guerilla war – even before going into production . . . For sheer incompatibility, the volatile cast of *Myra* is rivalled only by the Burton-Lyon-Gardner gallimaufry of *Night of the Iguana*. There is crustaceous veteran director, John Huston, portraying Uncle Buck Loner, the sagebrush sybarite. Huston, an inveterate cigar smoker, has been unhappy with a no-smoking clause that Mae West had written into her contract. There is the epicene Rex Reed, who eats peaches, scribbles notes for his book (about the making of *Myra*, naturally) and regularly breaks up the crew with his lavender drawl. Towering over all is the ribald old empress, Mae West, who threatens to steal the show as Leticia Van Allen, the drunken, horny agent.'

According to reports which emerged during the next nine tortuous months of making the movie (which ultimately cost in excess of $5 million), stage number six at Fox Studios which was used for shooting became known as 'The Contamination Area' while squabbles between the leading personalities raged daily. Raquel, though, was determined to succeed, and declared defiantly: 'There is no way that this is not going to be a good movie. I understand Myra thoroughly. I've always identified with her.'

The story concerns a male transvestite Myron (Rex Reed) who becomes Myra (Raquel) after a sex change operation. With his/her heart set on a career in Hollywood, Myra claims half of an acting school owned by Myron's uncle (John Huston) and then initiates a programme of sexually humiliating one of the pupils, Rusty Godowsky (Roger Herren). Her triumph is completed by foisting the unfortunate boy on a lecherous old talent agent (Mae West, 'The Queen of the Casting Couch') and then, reverting to a man once more, seducing his hapless girlfriend (Farrah Fawcett).

Three major elements emerged from Raquel's involvement with *Myra*. Her friendship with Rex Reed, her uneasy relationship with Mae West, and her defence of Mike Sarne who was to be savaged for his part in the movie.

Reed, who made his screen debut in the picture, said afterwards: 'There's no doubt Raquel enjoys being a film star because that's the only thing she ever wanted to be. But there are problems that go with being a star that she wasn't prepared for. Now she wants to be taken seriously as an actress, and nobody wants to take Raquel Welch seriously. Nobody wanted to take Jean Harlow seriously, or Monroe, and when Monroe tried to be serious that was the beginning of the end of her life. Raquel is a curious juxtaposition of Hollywood clichés. In New York I took her to the theatre one night. God knows how the word got out – maybe her own publicist did it – but there were photographers and TV cameras and reporters asking questions like, were she and I a new romance? We were mobbed, pushed up against the wall, and even when we got inside the theatre, during the performance, people were turning around and snapping pictures and asking for autographs. She seemed to adore all that. But later on I took her to dinner and she suddenly burst into tears, from the emotional exhaustion of the whole evening.'

Raquel's response to this was in keeping, and nicely judged the character of the remarkable New York writer and film critic: 'Yes, I adore Rex – but he's something like a pet cobra. I never knew which way he was going to swing. I could never tell when he was going to write an article and be slightly bitchy about me. I never really understood it, because he was always so sweet!'

Overleaf: The highly volatile cast of *Myra Breckinridge:* John Huston, Raquel, Mae West and Rex Reed

It was quite a different matter with Mae West. Before Raquel met Mae for the first time, she sent the seventy-seven-year-old former sex symbol who was making her return to the screen after twenty-six years, a huge bunch of flowers. She said she admired the older woman's ability and hoped for a good working relationship. Mae, however, arrived on the set amidst cheers, and 'pumped her elderly hips in a game imitation of her former self', to quote one report. She then informed Raquel: 'Honey, I used to have censor trouble when a man even sat on my lap. Since then I've had more men on my lap than table napkins.'

The atmosphere not surprisingly became highly charged. Raquel and Mae disputed the right to certain colour schemes in their outfits and both took up the cudgels over constant script changes. The film script was, allegedly, rewritten *ten times* before the picture was completed! In the end, the two actresses only appeared together on the screen on two occasions. Mae West commented rather tartly, 'Miss Welch is a sweet little thing. She has one or two scenes in the picture, I believe.' Raquel was, though, more ladylike: 'It was as though she was making an entirely different movie from me. But she is a very great lady and it has been a remarkable experience for me.'

Mike Sarne, at the heart of all the troubles, had begun the venture with very high hopes. 'My luck seemed to be in,' he said some years later. 'But the film was universally despised. My name soon spelt death in Hollywood. Still, it did make me $300,000.'

Speaking more specifically of the picture itself, he told Jack Bentley in February 1971: 'I meant the thing to be very funny, and I'm laughing at the critics who have taken it seriously. *Myra* is supposed to be satirical, a gigantic whack at all those complacent bloody people who run the film business.'

The critical reaction to the picture was, in actual fact, spectacularly varied. Donald Zec of the *Daily Mirror*, for instance, called it 'a truly nasty picture' and added, 'Whatever the distinguished writer Gore Vidal intended in his cynical and notorious book which gives the film its name, its translation to the screen succeeds only in giving good, honest dirt a bad name.' *Time* magazine thought it 'disgusting' and declared '*Myra Breckinridge* is about as funny as a child molester. It is an insult to intelligence, an affront to sensibility and an abomination to the eye. The result is an incoherent tale of sodomy, emasculation, auto-eroticism and plain bad taste.'

Two completely different publications found themselves as unlikely champions of the picture, however: the American pop culture's *Rolling Stone* and that ancient bastion of British traditions, *The Times*.

Wrote Michael Goodwin of *Rolling Stone*: '*Myra Breckinridge*, directed by Michael Sarne, isn't nearly as terrible as the unanimously bad reviews would lead you to believe. It isn't the best picture of the year, but it is far from the worst and I had a good time watching it. The film is a decent example of a genre of movies called *cinema maudit* (black movies) by the French critics – films without heroes, films which take an exceedingly dark view of the universe. If you are in a nasty enough mood, *Myra* is a right-on flick. It works from the inside. That is, it attempts to become the thing it is dissecting (in this case, Hollywood), and takes upon itself the very characteristic it wishes to deal with. Consequently, it is tasteless, offensive, shallow, self-indulgent, and it panders to the lowest level of audience expectations. Quite on purpose. The reverse double-whammy proved a little too tricky for most reviewers but maybe that makes it a better joke.'

The Times' John Russell Taylor also thought other critics had missed the point of the film. He declared: 'It was inevitable, no doubt, that any attempt to adapt Gore Vidal's classically un-adaptable novel (rivalled only by *Portnoy's Complaint*) should provide a ready-made field-day for connoisseurs of the cinematic bizarre. One cannot help wondering if producer Robert Fryer, who must have been well aware of what he was getting into, did not deliberately decide that in the circumstances the best thing – indeed the only thing – to do was to go for broke. Bizarre? All right, we'll show them bizarre! Now at last the film itself is unveiled. And – the biggest surprise of all – it is really rather good. Bizarre, certainly: it could hardly help being that. But more: it is a real film with a real idea.'

Russell Taylor also had praise for Mike Sarne's use of clips from old movies to underscore the Hollywood myth, then came to Raquel: 'Casting Raquel Welch as Myra proves a master-stroke: she is so obviously a whole lot of woman that one never doubts for a moment her ability to ride rough-shod over any mere man who gets in her way. And the rest of the cast do every-

The scene with Roger Herren (Rusty) which caused Raquel such heart-searching during the making of *Myra Breckinridge*

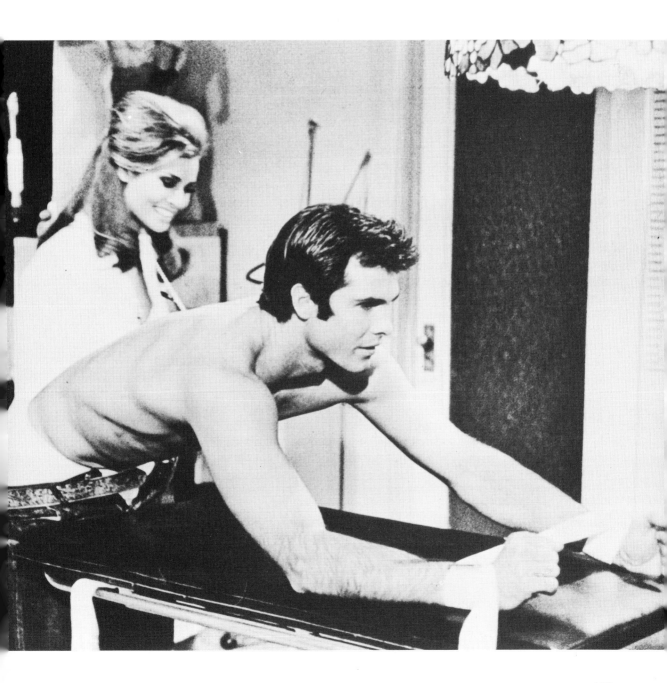

thing one could possibly expect of them, even if it is only sometimes to play second fiddle to the immortal shadows of Laurel and Hardy, Alice Faye and Shirley Temple. Perhaps Mrs Shirley Temple Black may feel that *Myra Breckinridge* is a pretty back-handed tribute to her legendary infant greatness: but for all that it is a real tribute, because a tribute wrung out of today's Hollywood, an admission that it can never be more than a pale reflection of its own heroic past.'

Undoubtedly one particular sequence in this picture had done much to draw the critics' wrath down on it. This became known as 'the famous buggery scene' in which Raquel as Myra humiliated Rusty Godowsky by thrusting a thermometer (seen) and then a dildo (not seen) between his buttocks and riding him like a cowboy at a rodeo. *Friends* magazine, which was not totally opposed to the film, commented: 'But we're obviously not quite ready to see the full thing, so the scene is fleshed out with shots of battering rams and castle gates, bursting dams, and rodeos, much like Hitchcock some time ago cutting from the beginning of a bedroom scene to a short of the train entering a tunnel.'

And of the performers, *Friends* had this to add: 'Although Raquel Welch lacks the steely, intellectual insane intensity of the original, she is passable, and anyway always good to look at. The same isn't true of the stiff, ageing, monotonous bulk of Mae West, who moves about like some tea-cosied Dalek delivering one awful unfunny line after another. She might be good for a fifteen-second spot on *Laugh-In* but any longer and the tedious sameness of her style and stance palls rapidly.'

Sensibly, Raquel avoided becoming too immersed in all the controversy. She told William Hall of the *Evening News* in October 1970: 'I realise that the picture deals with an unorthodox subject that might be offensive. I didn't only do it for sensation – I have a contract with Fox I have to fulfil. I'm very happy with the result and with my work in it.'

And when Michael Billington asked her six months later if she would make the picture again if asked to do so, she replied: 'Under the circumstances, yes. The only thing that worried me about it was the amount of preparation involved; but I dutifully went back and read about the lives of the forties stars and saw as many of their films again as I could. The film was a very good thing for me personally, but the script might have made Myra a much richer, fuller character and the fact that the director, Mike Sarne, was English meant – how shall I say? – that the sense of humour wasn't easily available to all.'

With the passage of time, Raquel has remained loyal to Sarne as well as to her conviction that *Myra Breckinridge* is a better film than many people have given it credit for being. This conviction was underlined in a remarkable interview with Andy Warhol in December 1974, when the experimental film-maker told Raquel he thought the picture was ahead of its time. 'In ten or twenty years,' Warhol said, 'I think *Myra Breckinridge* is going to be considered one of the best movies.'

He made a particular point of asking Raquel why she thought Mike Sarne had been so abused over the picture. 'He was treated very badly during the whole experience,' she replied. 'I mean he has a very good active wit, but he got to be quite abrasive after a while. Because every time he turned around somebody was confronting him with something. Either Rex had rewritten a scene, or Mae West had submitted some pages or other, I mean it was all banana time. And the poor guy, he wanted to treat it all as a great fun fantasy – he didn't want to explore the psychological motivations behind a transsexual. He just thought, "it's on another plane".'

Why had she wanted to play the part? Warhol asked. 'I got a really big hoot out of *Myra Breckinridge* when I read it at the time,' she said. 'And I really wanted to do it. Nobody understood why – because everybody thought it was really . . . awful. But it's a very funny role and there were some good scenes in it.'

Warhol took this opportunity to ask Raquel for her views on the controversial rape scene. 'The one thing I *didn't* think we should do graphically in the film was the seduction of Rusty Godowsky,' she said. 'Because there was all kinds of talk about how they were going to do it. And I said, "Look, Michael, you know, first of all forget all the devices and all the dildos and all that terrible shit. You've got to do it on a plane that's not upsetting. It shouldn't be shocking, it should be funny, and satirical, Myra should end up being this baton-twirling majorette, the

Americana-personified kind of thing.'' That's what the book represents in many ways, anyhow. I mean, sort of on a larger plane, he's doing a thing with a person who has trouble with his identity, sexually. But it's all about a much bigger thing. It's all about America and the way people get emasculated in this society, isn't it? You take it on to that plane of thinking.

'I admit I was always terrified of that scene – I never knew how he was going to do it. I mean,' she laughs, 'I knew how I was going to do it, and so it was going to have to be arm-twisting time. But I liked the way he shot it in the end, and I like that he accepted my ideas for it. Michael Sarne was an OK guy and I'd like to see him resurface.'

With hindsight, one can clearly see that *Myra Breckinridge* was an important film in Raquel's career. Among all the reviews with the cries of 'obscene', 'disastrous', even 'pornographic', ran the constant thread of praise for Raquel's performance. George Melly, Britain's abrasive critic of *The Observer*, spoke for the majority when he wrote that 'among the unfortunate cast, Raquel Welch proves that, given a passable part, she could be more than a fantasy lay.'

And at the New York premiere for the picture in June 1970, while Mae West was delivering homilies on the secret of sex appeal ('Eat fresh fruits and vegetables, don't drink or smoke, and sex will take care of itself') Raquel talked quietly to pressmen about her image and her future. 'I realise my image put me where I am,' she said, 'or I wouldn't be able to complain about it. But I think all sex goddesses have basically been unhappy. I know we sound like ungracious asses, but it's like being a shell and I'm tired of it. People don't think I have ability, and I think they are wrong. I've tried to fight it. Marilyn couldn't fight it because she wasn't strong enough. Well I am, and I think I can lick it.'

And she continued with feeling: 'I'll continue working and trying. There's quite a bit more that can be asked of me that I can do much better work than I've ever done. So take my word for it, I'm going to pursue singing and dancing as well as serious acting. I probably won't ever be Barbra Streisand – but then again she'll definitely never be me, either, will she?'

Just one of Raquel's several stunning appearances at the Oscar ceremonies in Hollywood – here with Gene Hackman and Cloris Leachman

Overleaf: Raquel as a peasant girl in *The Beloved* (1970)

110

Raquel was as good as her word, too, for while *Myra Breckinridge* alternately intrigued or revolted audiences around the world (except in Australia where it was banned), she went into rehearsal for her first hour-long television special, *Raquel*, sponsored by Coca-Cola for showing on CBS.

On 7 April 1970 she took a break to appear at the 42nd Annual Academy Awards Ceremony at the Dorothy Chandler Pavilion in Los Angeles. Asked to present the Oscar for special effects, she gave the audience one of the best moments of humour during the evening – at her own expense. Looking stunning in a low-cut evening dress, she leant forward provocatively over the lectern and announced she had been asked to present 'the special visual effects award'. She paused, flashed a knowing smile and then added, 'and there are two of them'. The *double entendre* brought a roar of approval from the star-studded audience.

'Who said this dame was dumb?' one dinner-jacketed movie mogul was heard to chuckle behind his huge cigar.

The television spectacular *Raquel* went out three weeks later on 26 April. It had been given one of the highest ever budgets for a single show and she herself was being paid $400,000. More importantly, the show was made under the auspices of Curtwel, with Patrick acting as producer.

The theme was simple: a world tour with Raquel singing, dancing and acting against the backdrop of some of the most exotic locations on the globe. The itinerary took in London (where she also found time to tape a guest spot on *The Tom Jones Show* for ATV), France, Portugal, Mexico and California – all to 'match her spectacular beauty with some of the world's finest beauty spots' – according to a CBS press handout. The guest stars were John Wayne, Bob Hope and Tom Jones, while among her own contributions Raquel injected a little topicality into the proceedings with a takeoff of Mae West.

Predictably, the show attracted high audience ratings in America where the quality and general slickness of production was praised by most of the critics, although some found the rapid cutting and bizarre camera angles somewhat annoying.

Ben Gross of the *New York Daily News* gave the special begrudging praise, but remarked that 'instead of titling it *Raquel*, the ingenious fellows who devise the come-ons for attractions should have called it *Travels with the Body Beautiful*, for the show roamed over many beautiful spots of America and Europe, each serving as the background for a gal generously endowed with visible charm.' When the show turned up for screening in Britain two months later by the BBC (who apparently paid £8,500 for the privilege) Ken Bailey of *The People* declared that Raquel 'comes over as a very amusing personality', and he could well understand why 'it has already paid off with bookings around the world'.

The success of the TV special was all the encouragement Patrick and Raquel needed to go ahead with their long-held plans to make a full-length picture with her own company. Now that Raquel had fulfilled her obligations to Twentieth Century-Fox, there was nothing to stand in their way.

Patrick took the opportunity to talk about Curtwel and its objectives to the press. 'What makes it tick? I'll tell you,' he said. 'It is the fact that in the film business our names are bankable and everyone sweats. We all swim or we all sink together. Nobody gets ahead in the company. We all share together from the first dollar.'

Curtis said that the company didn't have any fixed pattern of operating or raising money. The approach to finance was flexible; the only constant factor was promotion and publicity. 'That is the key. I watch over every still that goes out.'

Curtwel worked on the basis of both partners agreeing to do something, he said, if they disagreed, Raquel was free to go off and do her own thing. So far they hadn't disagreed.

Patrick Curtis claimed that Raquel's seven films for Fox had so far grossed $125 million, and she personally was worth over $4 million. As the prime asset of Curtwel (which itself had fluid assets of $2,500,000) she was an attractive figure – in more ways than one – when it came to raising finance for a new project.

The picture which Curtwel had chosen for their debut was *The Beloved*, a stark and emotional drama set on the island of Cyprus. It was budgeted to cost half a million dollars, said Curtis, and he had already sold it to MGM for $1 million without them seeing a foot of film or a single still. 'We told them

what we were doing,' he said. 'They sent back thirteen sugges-
tions of one sentence each, most of which we had already done.'

With this kind of support, Curtis was full of optimism when
he set off for Cyprus. 'At the moment Curtwel is us,' he added,
'Raquel more than me. But we will spread.'

The Beloved had been written by George Pan Cosmatos, a
twenty-nine-year-old Greek, who had worked as an assistant
director on the famous movie, *Zorba the Greek*, and was now to
have his own chance to direct. Although the story was modern in
setting it had strong overtones of Greek tragedy. Raquel played
a young wife who falls in love with her husband's best friend
(Richard Johnson) who has just returned to the island after
fifteen years in exile. The film called for her to do away with all
the glamour and stunning costumes which had been such a feature of her earlier movies, and instead pull her shoulder-length
hair into a severe bun and wear the simple peasant dresses of a
Cypriot village girl. 'I could hardly bear to put them on at the
beginning,' she confessed, 'they were so dowdy and shapeless.
But I got over that, and of course they made the demands of the
part more exacting still.'

Travelling to Cyprus, Raquel did her homework on the
island, reading up on the people and getting particular enjoyment from two books, *Bitter Lemons* and *The Birth of Aphrodite*.
Although she was based at the luxurious Hilton Hotel in
Nicosia, shooting took place a forty-minute drive away at the
remote mountain village of Karmi (population 400), which was
soon nicknamed by the crew 'Karmi Sutra' – not altogether
because of Raquel's presence but also because the temperature
remained relentlessly above 100 degrees.

Her arrival naturally generated stories and headlines galore.
The *Sunday Times*' foreign correspondent, David Leith, leading
the vanguard on 16 August 1970: 'The temperature was
running at a sweltering 108 degrees this week as Miss Raquel
Welch erupted on the island of Cyprus with the exquisite subtlety
of a fifty calibre machine-gun. Some meteorologists claimed the
heatwave came from a hot front over the East Mediterranean,
and was unconnected with the superstar's descent, but this view
was largely discounted in the remote village of Karmi, where she

is making a film called *The Beloved*. Here the mere mention of her name was enough to make the locals gulp, sweat, and rapidly call for more iced Coca-Cola.'

Leith found director George Pan Cosmatos confirming Raquel's stated intention of taking more demanding roles. 'This film is going to be a breakthrough,' he said. 'Before, no one has expected her to do anything more difficult than hold a horse and pant rhythmically. In this film she has to express sexual frustration, love, hope and ultimately death.'

Before work began, Raquel had a meeting with the President of Cyprus, Archbishop Makarios, who jokingly asked why the film wasn't being shot at Paphos. He told her this was reputed to be the birthplace of the goddess Aphrodite – but what he didn't add was that legend claims that any woman who bathes there is given the gift of renewing her virginity.

The press and photographers trailed Raquel relentlessly during the filming, and although she granted several interviews, she was less than amused by persistent enquiries from *The Sun*. Husband Patrick finally non-plussed the paper's reporter when he enquired of Raquel, 'What are your statistics?' Quick as a flash Patrick responded, 'Adequate.'

She was more forthcoming to Bill Hall of the *Evening News* who asked about what he saw as 'the deglamourisation of the world's number one sex goddess'.

'It's no gimmick, I assure you,' Raquel said. 'I'm not turning my back on anything. I'm not out to crack an image, because first labels always stick anyway, whatever you do. I'll always be a sex symbol to some people. I'd just like to show them I can act as well. That's why I'm here. But I don't worry about being a sex symbol any more. None of the things I do has any great significance. Most of what I've done is ultimately forgettable.

'Women,' she went on, 'are always thought of as just so much ass. I don't mind it. But when you're a sex goddess people treat you as though you have no integrity. I mean, they actually expect me to have affairs and things.'

Curiously, those words were to take on a significant ring in the next few months . . .

Thomas Luther Price (Robert Culp), she learns to handle a ·45 revolver and sets out on a one-woman mission to revenge herself on the killers. Driven on by the belief that: 'There aren't any hard women, only soft men', she remorselessly tracks down the brothers: gunning one in a brothel, another in a perfume store and the third in a deserted prison.

Yet again an enduring image of Raquel was used in the promotion of the film. When she flees from her flaming homestead all she has on is a poncho and this she uses to distract attention from the gun concealed on her naked hip beneath. It proves to be the one vital statistic her enemies don't notice.

The critics were generally not impressed with *Hannie Caulder*, and *Time* continued its verbal bashing of Raquel: 'As has been amply proved in the past,' said the magazine, 'Miss Welch's acting ability is greatly overshadowed by her endowments.'

Arthur Thirkell of the *Daily Mirror* thought differently, though. '*Hannie Caulder* is quite an impressive Western,' he said. 'Exciting, well acted – and I include Miss Welch.' Patrick Gibbs of the *Daily Telegraph* was, as usual, considered in his judgement and felt that a fine opportunity had been missed by the picture in not making enough of some elements of burlesque in the story. 'If the burlesquing of the baddies which takes place – as well as that of some supine sheriffs – had been extended to Hannie and Price then this film might have approached the success of *Cat Balou* in this line; but the scriptwriter, Z. X. Jones and director Burt Kennedy, get bogged down for long passages in a pseudo-romantic style which gives Miss Welch few chances to display, along with her legs, her usual sense of fun.'

If new elements to Raquel's screen character were being discovered all the time, none of them matched the surprise which greeted the news of her separation from Patrick on 12 April 1971. True, there had been rumours in some of the more outrageous film star magazines and scandal sheets that Raquel was becoming fed up with the amount of work her husband was lining up for her, but she had countered these stories with a press statement, 'This trouble is nothing we can't work out.'

But, according to their public relations man, Warren Cowan,

An absolutely enchanting shot from *Fuzz* with Raquel playing Detective Eileen McHenry

they evidently had been unable to work them out. 'Raquel and Patrick have been having marital problems,' he said in Hollywood. 'They have not decided yet what to do about them, and will no doubt be considering that in the next few weeks.' He added that Patrick had moved out of the couple's Beverly Hills home leaving behind the collection of cars he had assembled – including a Ferrari, dune buggy, Eldorado and two Rolls Royces – but as yet no decision had been made about a divorce.

The news made headlines around the world. Although Raquel was to continue working for the rest of the year, the parting from Patrick overshadowed everything else. Finally, on 2 September, she announced that she had started proceedings and filed a divorce suit in the Los Angeles Superior Court. 'I felt trapped in the marriage,' she said simply. 'I couldn't combine being a housewife, actress, sex symbol and a mother.'

At the time, Raquel was not prepared to discuss her marriage to Patrick Curtis, but a year later had distanced herself enough from the events to make this fairminded assessment of their time together: 'I'm not going to start rapping Patrick,' she said. 'I don't know how to say it, but there was always another side of every question that he always stood for. We disagreed quite strenuously over a lot of things. I once felt he knew more than I did and I had no confidence in myself at all. A husband has a tremendous influence and if you let him make all the decisions you lose your ability to make your own.

'When you cease being tremendously excited by somebody you may still enjoy and respect him but you may not have a lot in common with him any more. In the kind of business I'm in, there's always a refurbishing of yourself. You travel along a certain line, and then you say "OK, I'm sick of this. I want to do something else. I want to rethink and revitalise my interest in things I'm doing." But the person you're living with may have a resistance to this and you can't bring him along with you. He's gone off in a different way.'

Raquel was quite prepared to accept that she must have become hard to live with as she became unhappy. 'I'm sure I must have been a shrew,' she said. 'I get pretty quiet when I'm really unhappy. I think I can take a lot of abuse from any situation, or any one person, before I blow my top. When I finally get mad it's usually for all the wrong reasons – and whack! That's it. It's like at last having an excuse to say what you really wanted to say for ages. I've got to learn to speak up for myself much earlier on in the game.'

She also revealed that she made no attempt to conceal what was happening from her children, Damon and Tahnee, to whom Patrick had been closer than their real father, James Welch. 'I think children are very resilient and adaptable to change,' Raquel said. 'I certainly talked with enough doctors and psychologists about the effects of divorce on my children. After all, I've been divorced twice and I'm concerned about what happens to them. Some people think they should hold down a marriage or a job that makes them miserable for their children's sake. But I find that if you tell the children what's happening and explain your decisions, you usually get their full support. I told Damon and Tahnee right away. I didn't let them try to figure it out for themselves and perhaps worry about whether something might be their fault. They said, ''That's OK, Mom.'' That didn't mean they were happy about it all. It just meant it was OK. Just that. Not the end of the world.'

Was she now opposed to marriage? she was asked. 'Well, I am just not equipped to deal with an existence that involves one particular person all the time,' she replied. 'Even though I have outside work and outside interests I still want to be free to do what I want to do and I don't want to have to make excuses to anybody. I guess that's pretty selfish but that's the way I feel.'

Patrick Curtis has also been able to reflect on his extraordinary marriage, although some of his conclusions differ from those of his ex-wife. Talking to Fiona Macdonald Hull in 1978 he said: 'Raquel is a very closed person, and I never realised things were stewing up inside her. For her, work finished when she walked off the set. But I brought my problems home and I got mad a lot and did a lot of yelling and screaming. I'm sorry about that now because she couldn't have been expected to understand.'

Curtis believed it was true that he had manipulated Raquel during the ten years they were together. 'But it was never done with any malice,' he said. 'I had more experience than she had in the movie business and I wanted to protect her. Even today, though I'm married again, I still talk daily to her on the phone. I know she is a very lonely lady. After the divorce she went for nearly a year without dating anybody. The phone just didn't ring. What man is going to have the guts to call up Raquel Welch and ask her out to dinner? I think the situation is much the same today. She's lonely, she has nobody to take care of her and a lot of people have tried to use her. Basically, she's a very vulnerable person, a woman caught up in a difficult world.'

Raquel agrees that it was difficult to adjust to being a single woman after having been with Patrick for so long. 'I literally couldn't get myself out of the house,' she recalls. 'I'd always had somebody around who said, ''This is the way you're to look, this is what to say, these are the people we like.'' Then, suddenly, there was no one there to tell me and I thought I'd fall flat on my face and make a fool of myself.'

Raquel knew only too well that many other film stars faced with similar situations had retreated into alcohol or drugs. She knew the dangers and decided on psychoanalysis. It helped her enormously to readjust. 'I didn't date for a long time because I really didn't want to,' she says. 'I was invited to several parties and I could hardly get in the door. I thought I wouldn't be able to say ''good evening'' right. I wondered what I could talk about if I got into a sexual discussion. What was I going to do or say? Fantasies of dark doom took over. It doesn't worry me any longer. I think people are generally frightened of a lot of other people they don't know. Then, you begin to realise there are some people there at these parties who had *also* sat home and thought, ''How am I going to get through the front door?'' I went first to a couple of big parties given by good friends. Once I got inside, I didn't have time to think of bad happenings. I was drinking, having a good time, feeling relaxed, even dancing, and meeting all kinds of people. It all seemed to take care of itself. I didn't have to sit by the wall. I've finally relaxed enough to know that people aren't really out to get you. If you accept certain things about yourself, they accept them too. You really don't have to work at impressing everybody all the time.'

Surely the most beautiful nun ever in *Bluebeard* (1971)

As the trauma of the break-up of her marriage faded, Raquel continued to fulfil her movie commitments. For Universal Artists she put in nine days work in Hollywood filming a cameo part in *Fuzz*; flew to Budapest to appear as one of the mass-murderer's wives in Alexander Salkind's *Bluebeard*, and then played the *Kansas City Bomber* for her own company. Each picture added a little to the problems she had endured off-screen.

In *Fuzz* Raquel was reunited with Burt Reynolds whom she had previously appeared with in *100 Rifles*. Now, though, Reynolds was a star and took the central part of Detective Steve Carella, a member of Boston's 87th Precinct, hot on the trail of a series of bizarre killings and a murderer demanding $50,000 to stop his attacks on local officials. Raquel was detective Eileen McHenry, assigned to catch a rapist who is prowling the parks while all this is going on. Also in the cast was Yul Brynner as the mysterious 'Deaf Man', Jack Weston as Burt Reynolds' partner, and Tom Skerritt who was involved in one of the funniest moments in the picture when he and Raquel become entangled in a sleeping bag while pretending to be lovers keeping an eye out for the rapist.

Raquel and Burt Reynolds had not got on well when making their previous picture together, nor did they this time. She was upset by some of his remarks on the set and when he appeared on television. The final straw came over her billing in the picture and the publicity pictures of her which were being released to promote it. She therefore refused to play any part in exploiting the movie.

Reynolds told his interviewer: 'Let's be honest about it, Raquel's not one of my favourite people in the world. I don't consider her a warm and sensitive young lady. And she doesn't have much affection for me. She has had a strange career. She gets blasted critically, and I think she has built up a kind of wall around herself. She is gorgeous, though. God or somebody did a hell of a job.'

Reynolds was wrong about her getting blasted by the critics, however. For her role in *Fuzz*, several critics had nothing but praise. Clive Hirschhorn of the *Sunday Express* said that 'Miss Welch's shapely presence breezes airily through the 87th

A dramatic moment from *Kansas City Bomber*, one of the toughest and most gruelling films Raquel has ever made

Precinct like a cool wind in August and puts every man in a holiday mood.' While Felix Barker of the *Evening News* declared that he 'never expected to see Raquel Welch as a police detective investigating a rape', and found her performance 'endearing because in most movies American cops take themselves so very seriously.'

Budapest in Hungary where Raquel went to shoot her next picture, *Bluebeard*, proved a long way from Boston both in terms of distance and her relationship with the star of the picture, Richard Burton. She was cast as Magdalena, a nymphomaniac nun, one of several women who try to seduce the much-married 'Bluebeard' of the title, an Austrian nobleman, Baron von Sepper, played by Burton. For her endeavour she is suffocated alive in a coffin.

Raquel found the experience of going behind the Iron Curtain for the first time an extraordinary one. 'Budapest was great,' she recalled later, 'but it's an occupied country, and we had this Comrade Julie with us the whole time. She was really dyed-in-the-wool and everything had to go through her to get done. So if you wanted to have some Kodak film developed, you had to say,

''We know that the Communists can do this better than anyone in the world and we need this by three o'clock this afternoon. So do you think . . . ?'' It was really quite a scene trying to get this ''comrade'' to do her stuff. It was funny what people had to go through in their manner toward her to get her to think she wasn't doing something Capitalistic, but that she was proving that the State could supply these ''necessities''. It was really funny.'

Raquel was also present for the huge party thrown in the city to mark Elizabeth Taylor's fortieth birthday. 'It was just kind of crazy,' she said. 'There were people showing up from all over the world. Princess Grace was there, and Ringo Starr and all sorts of people whose names I can't remember. There were just hundreds of luminescent people. And there in the middle was Richard in his gold lamé polo shirt and Elizabeth with thousands of gardenias in her hair and white kaftans and flowing chiffon. I just wore a little dress, a thing I got in Beverly Hills. It was a very pretty dress . . . but all the time I just thought how crazy it all was!'

According to Mary Bredin, who was Raquel's secretary from 1968 to 1977, and was with her in Budapest, Raquel met Richard Burton for the first time at this party. The two superstars were instantly attracted to one another, she says. 'One of the biggest affairs of Raquel's life, although it lasted only three days, was her fling with Richard Burton,' she said in 1978. 'It may have been brief, but it was very passionate. On the first day of filming, Elizabeth was on the set watching, but then Richard's brother died and he flew to Britain for the funeral. He returned the next day – without Elizabeth. And immediately he started flirting with Raquel. He invited her to his caravan for lunch and tea – and for champagne every time there was a break in filming. Raquel was absolutely dazzled. ''He's so intellectual,'' she said.'

According to Mary Bredin the affair continued by post for about two months after the film was finished, after which Burton's letters ceased. By then Raquel had left Beverly Hills once more for Oregon to work on a new picture, *Kansas City Bomber*.

The origins of this film about the peculiarly American 'sport' of roller derbies were unusual to say the least. Raquel was used to receiving fan letters – estimates have put the figure as high as half a million of them a year during the late sixties and early seventies – but to receive a thesis on her life and career, plus a script designed specifically for her to star in, was something rather different.

Yet this is precisely what a young Los Angeles undergraduate named Barry Sandler presented her with in 1972. Sandler was a devoted admirer and had written the thesis as part of his course at the University of Southern California. He had also had the idea for a film about the life of a 'roller derby queen'. Rather than entrust his precious manuscript to the post, Sandler delivered the script to Raquel's home. Unfortunately she was out at the time, but a maid took Barry's script in and later began idly flipping through the pages. After a while she was hooked on the story, and when Raquel returned urged her to read it.

Raquel liked it, too. And with some extra work by professional screenwriters Thomas Rickman and Calvin Clements, *Kansas City Bomber* was born. Raquel decided on producing it herself in conjunction with Jules Levy and Arthur Gardner, MGM handling the distribution.

Talking about the picture after its completion, she said, 'It was my property and so I had real interest in its growth from start to finish. I guess it was just native instinct that attracted me to it in the first place. I've always felt I could be good in an action-type part. I really had to work hard on it. I had to undergo months of skate training – which often left me black and blue – as well as learning the intricacies that go to make up a roller derby. I actually fell and broke my wrist during the shooting!

'It seemed relevant to me to put a woman in the athletic area in this particular age when women are changing their role. I am not very moved by women's changing role, though. It is something that happens very slowly and doesn't particularly wrench me. It might not be progress. It might be regression, you know.

'I just think women are people and should have as many possibilities as men do. They should be able to do what they want with their own lives and follow instincts and their own needs. I like to think I am following MY own instincts!'

Raquel played K. C. Carr, an ambitious roller derby star who is forced to leave Kansas City and carve a new place for herself in a team called the Portland Loggers run by the ruthless Burt Henry (Kevin McCarthy). Here she is forced to battle both on the boards and off them with the local favourites, Jackie Burdette (Helena Kallianiotes), and Horrible Hank Hopkins (Norman Alden) as well as making peace with her two estranged children (a very young Jodie Foster and Stephen Manley) before scoring her ultimate triumph in what is billed as 'the match race of the century'.

Raquel's faith in the picture and her hard work in making it were amply rewarded with the most universally favourable reviews she had ever received. The much respected Thomas Berger of *Esquire* who confessed that he had 'never previously looked at Miss Welch in anything but still photographs', declared: 'She seems spiritually altogether at home in the role and is an actress sufficient to the day thereof, a good deal better, indeed, than I should snobbishly have supposed.'

Margaret Hinxman in the *Sunday Telegraph* joined the applause, calling *Kansas City Bomber* 'a strong, gutsy attempt from Raquel Welch to play a real character rather than a screen sex symbol.' And Arthur Thirkell in the *Daily Mirror*, by now a confirmed admirer, went further: 'I happen to think that Miss Welch has a lot to offer in films. She's an intelligent girl, whose acting is underrated.'

William Paul in New York's *Village Voice* capped them all with a piece that must have found pride of place in Raquel's scrapbook in August 1972. Complimenting director Jerrold Freedman for the 'documentary feel' of much of his footage of the aggressive, no-holds-barred world of roller derbies (much of it was, indeed, shot in real-life locations), he welcomed what he saw as the return of a special kind of woman: '*Kansas City Bomber* is worth seeing,' he wrote, 'if only because its central character marks a return to the kind of independent, self-aware professional woman that, as Molly Haskell has rightly observed, has practically disappeared from contemporary movies. That's precisely the kind of role that some of the brightest screen

Raquel with Barry Sandler, the fan who wrote the story of *Kansas City Bomber* for her

personalities of the thirties and forties used to build careers on, and if this new film and *Hannie Caulder* are any indication, Welch herself seems to have decided on this route. While Welch is hardly in a league with Barbara Stanwyck, Katharine Hepburn, Rosalind Russell, or even Joan Crawford, one of the nicest surprises about *Kansas City Bomber* is how close she comes to bringing off her role. In her bigger dramatic moments here she seems less of a mannequin than ever before, more emotionally committed, giving conviction to the almost playful fierceness of a gum-chewing screaming match with another derby star or to the helplessness in confronting a young son hopelessly estranged from her by her career.

'The central characters in both *Hannie Caulder* and *Kansas City Bomber*, in their respective searches for independence, provided potential for two of the most interesting women's roles of the year. And if Welch can ever get into her performances more of the sensitivity and sensibility with which she chooses her roles, she might yet emerge as one of the major actresses of the seventies.'

The film itself also provided a bonus in that she had begun a new, warm relationship, with the picture's costume designer, Ronald Talsky, a bearded, darkly handsome young man.

Raquel felt she could face the future with optimism now that the failure of her marriage was behind her. She could even tell Kenneth Bailey with a smile in September 1972 as she celebrated her thirty-second birthday, 'I intend to retire at forty-five anyway.'

Unhappily, trouble with fellow actors and producers lay once more just around the corner, compounded with charges of assault and battery and even a bomb threat . . .

Bruises and a broken wrist were among Raquel's souvenirs from *Kansas City Bomber!*

8 Explosive Times

WHEN RAQUEL LEFT for the French Riviera in October 1972 to begin work on her next picture, *The Last of Sheila*, the quietly-spoken Ron Talsky was by her side. During the filming of *Kansas City Bomber*, on which he was the costume designer, Ron had made himself invaluable to her with his painstaking work on her outfits as well as his generally helpful and considerate attitude. He was a complete contrast to so many of the hyped-up and hectic young men Raquel usually met when filming, and a relationship began to develop, although she later admitted she had not been immediately attracted to him.

Raquel was, in fact, cagey about her personal life when talking to writer Stephen Birmingham before travelling to France. Because of who she was, she said, 'The men I date have to be men who have achieved something in their own right.' She went on: 'I have very few friends, you see, and there is no serious love in my life at the moment. I don't think I'm ever going to marry again. Working as hard as I have, and living like a nun for as long as I have, I've just never made many friends.'

Raquel confided that she could number one famous film star among her friends, Cary Grant, and that he had recently invited her to lay the cornerstone of a resort-hotel complex he was developing in Ireland. Only her film commitments prevented her taking up an invitation she would have thoroughly enjoyed.

The Last of Sheila was a murder mystery among the Hollywood set in which she co-starred with a group of leading actors including the Americans Richard Benjamin, Dyan Cannon, James Coburn and Joan Hackett and two Englishmen, James Mason and Ian McShane. The script was by two leading film world luminaries, writer-composer Stephen Sondheim and actor Anthony Perkins, and described the activities of a wealthy and unpleasant movie producer called Clinton (James Coburn) who organises some sinister 'games' on his yacht and gets murdered for his pains. His guests are then faced with investigating each other's dirty secrets to try and discover who among them is the killer. Director of the picture being made for Warner Bros was Herbert Ross, a man with several successes to his name including *Goodbye, Mr Chips* and *The Owl and the Pussycat*.

The omens for the picture were not good from the start. The

Raquel looking a little like Garbo as she arrives in London in November 1972 during her troubles making *The Last of Sheila* normally sun-scorched Riviera was deluged by storms and for some days the schedule looked under threat. Then, on the night of 9 October, an even more serious threat put the entire picture at risk as well as the lives of three of the stars.

This night of drama far more vivid than any scriptwriter might have dreamed up, began at 9 p.m. with a telephone call to the police station at Villefranche. The cast of *The Last of Sheila* were at that moment filming a night scene in a café in the town. Dyan Cannon, James Coburn, James Mason and Joan Hackett had actually just completed their parts and left the set – leaving behind Richard Benjamin, Ian McShane and Raquel to finish the scene.

The phone call to the police claimed to be on behalf of the Black September terrorist group. The caller said a bomb had been planted in the café and would be detonated unless everyone left. The reason for this threat, said the voice on the line, was because 'there are too many Jewish people involved in the film'.

News of the threat was immediately relayed to the set and police reinforcements and plain clothes detectives were hurried there. The crowd of sightseers who had gathered in the little palm-lined square to watch the filming inside the café were dispersed, while all the traffic in the neighbourhood was diverted. A vigorous search for clues was mounted, and experts began to comb the café for any sign of the bomb.

Director Herbert Ross immediately called a halt to shooting and informed Raquel and her two male co-stars what had happened. As the search continued, Ross told his actors as well as the camera crew and technicians that a decision would have to be made whether or not to defy the threat. For the next two hours everyone withdrew a hundred yards from the café and left the police to their work. It was an anxious time for everyone.

Richard Benjamin was the first to take direct action. He told the other actors and members of the film unit: 'It could be a great personal tragedy if we carry on, but I don't think we should pay attention to the call. If we stop now we might as well stop the film completely, otherwise this will happen every day.'

Ian McShane also told the crew, made up of Britons, Americans and French, 'I don't think we should stop work. I am prepared to carry on.' Raquel, too, spoke to the assembled company, 'I have to admit I'm very nervous. But I will go on if everyone else will.'

Herbert Ross made an immediate decision to phone a top Warner Bros executive in Hollywood, Richard Shephard, to explain what had happened. Shephard assured him that the studio would abide by whatever decision he made on the spot. It was a tense situation as the minutes ticked away on the still brightly-lit, but now completely silent, location. The eyes of all the members of the film team looked from one to another as the need for a decision became even more pressing. With the passing minutes, the fear which grew strongest was that the Black September movement might have decided on a policy of harassment of film locations in many places, and this might just be the first 'test' case. There was, of course, the danger that the threat was real – but to capitulate now would undoubtedly have endless repercussions.

The stars and crew decided to carry on. For Raquel in particular the next few hours were among the most frightening of her life. She was at the very centre of the action in the café, in the most exposed position, and had to go back into the glare of the battery of arc lights and continue with her part as if nothing was going on outside the drama of the story she was acting. 'I'll never be quite sure how I got through the rest of that scene,' she said later. 'But I was glad when we finished at 3 a.m. as scheduled. I was mighty glad, too, that the threat seemed to have been a hoax.'

To look now at the scene in *The Last of Sheila*, aware of the atmosphere that surrounded the shooting, makes Raquel's performance all the more creditable, Ken Adam, the designer of the film, later declared that night to be one of the most dramatic he had been involved in – and that included the several James Bond films he worked on!

A week later the unit ran into troubles again – though with the weather this time. An almost gale-force storm blew up while they were filming at a ruined monastery on an island just off Cannes. The night of 17 October proved a wild one; Raquel had been reluctant to leave the comfort of her hotel at Vence, high in the mountains behind Nice. She only had a small caravan in which to hide from the fury of the storm which lashed the ruins. She might also have been excused for thinking that she had somehow upset the ancient gods of nature by visiting this island where women are not traditionally allowed to go.

A patient London journalist, John Robbins, who had been trying to see Raquel during her work on *The Last of Sheila* finally met her on this inhospitable night. The weather and the demands of her role naturally dominated their conversation. 'Acting-wise it hasn't been as physically tough as *Hannie Caulder* and *Kansas City Bomber*,' she said, 'they were much tougher. But the rain hasn't helped you know. This gorgeous, glamorous picture in the wonderful sunny Côte d'Azur has turned out to be a bit of a splodge. This is not my idea of spending an enjoyable evening, but they're paying you the money so you have to do it. I just hope for some time to eat and sleep! If I have to do a scene in the rain and cold and late at night, I just go ahead and do it and don't complain.'

Raquel told Robbins that her part in the picture as Alice, a movie actress as distinct from a movie queen, was not one she had picked. 'It was something, as a working actress, I have fitted into my schedule between *Bomber* and my live appearances at Las Vegas.'

She went on: 'I would say I am very professional in my attitude towards work . . . I don't worry a lot, but I suppose I would if this film was particularly important to me. I know I am doing a good job, but I can't say what the film is going to be like. It's not my responsibility in its entirety. It's one of those pictures which relies on how the culminated efforts of several hundred people work out. Yes, in some respects I am a team person. Everybody enjoys being a part of a good team. I don't enjoy being associated with anything in a perpetual state of chaos. We are all individuals, but we are in a business in which we all depend on other people. Personally, I think I am a very easy person to work with because I know my job. I come in on time and I don't make a fuss about things.'

These were strangely prophetic words in the light of what suddenly exploded on the front pages of the world's press on the

Raquel with Ron Talsky in 1974

141

morning of 8 November. SAD RAQUEL IN TEARS AFTER
BIG FILM ROW – headlined the *Daily Mirror* and reported:
'Raquel Welch flew into London in tears yesterday after a
violent row with film director Herbert Ross. The film row flared
up in Nice where Raquel stormed off the set of *The Last of Sheila*.

'Her co-star James Mason said in an astonishing attack:
''She is the most selfish, ill-mannered, inconsiderate actress that
I've ever had the displeasure of working with. She flew into a
tantrum when she was told she couldn't go to London for the
opening of one of her films. People pleaded with her, but the
tantrum continued. Herbert Ross is an excellent friend and a
very talented man who is extremely patient, but not surprisingly
he cracked.'''

A friend flying with Raquel said that she was 'absolutely
exhausted' and was cancelling plans she had made to appear on
the Michael Parkinson chat show. Of James Mason's comments
she would only say, 'I consider them beneath contempt.'

The following day Raquel flew back to Nice to shoot the final
scenes of the picture. Warner Bros, however, issued a statement
to the newspapers which were, naturally, bristling with rumour
and speculation. The statement read: 'We have read the comments of Raquel Welch about her difficulties with *The Last of
Sheila* production in Nice. We wish to say only that we are
delighted with the production and direction of the picture by
Herbert Ross, and by the splendid performance of an outstand-
ing cast. Our only disappointment is with the behaviour of Miss
Welch and her public utterances. Nonetheless, she has completed her performance and, happily, our production has now
resumed in a professional manner.'

To this a Warner Bros official added: 'What we are objecting
to is her remarks about the production being behind schedule
and over budget.'

On her return to Nice, Raquel was besieged by reporters
who asked if she had walked off the set because of a row with
James Mason. 'It was nothing to do with him,' she said. 'But
my lawyer has told me not to divulge the real reason.'

The following day the saga came to a halt when Raquel
announced that she had instructed her lawyers to file a suit for

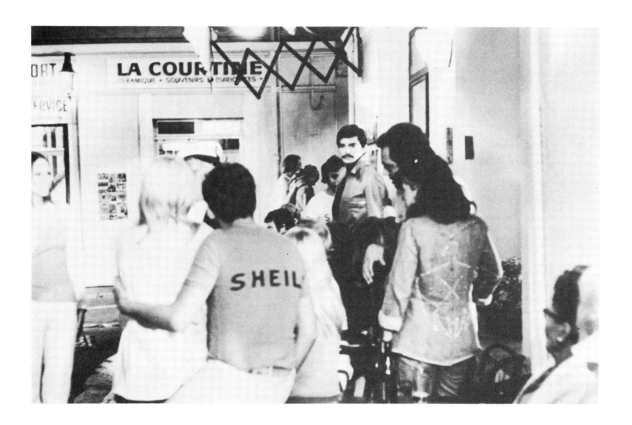

A candid shot of the cafe location during the bomb threat to the making of *The Last of Sheila*

alleged assault and battery over an incident in her dressing-room while filming *The Last of Sheila*. The suit, against Herbert Ross, was to be filed in Los Angeles. Her statement added: 'I have never in twenty-one films walked out or quit any movie. I justifiably fled to London to escape physical harm.'

The Last of Sheila had certainly lead a chequered life in the making, and perhaps not surprisingly generally fared badly at the hands of the critics. Jack Tinker of the *Daily Mail* called it 'the most ghastly yacht-party ever devised', while David Robinson in *The Times* declared it 'a sub-Agatha Christie intrigue about a party game that turns to murder, worked out in tortuous detail with all the crazed ingenuity of a lunatic

Raquel did not allow the terrorist threat to *The Last of Sheila* affect her performance

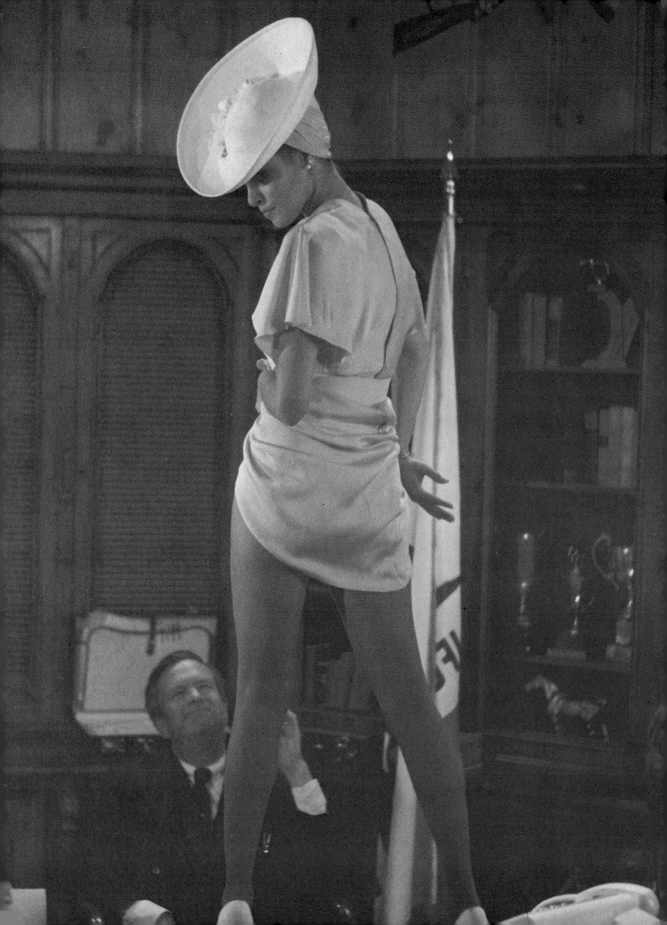

unravelling string.' And of the cast themselves, he added: 'This very weight of talent seems only to add to the offence.'

Only Stephen Farber had kind words for the picture and its actors. 'It is a stylish, literate, exceptionally entertaining diversion in the classic tradition of the good-bad movie. It combines two hardy but unfashionable genres – the whodunit and the Hollywood exposé . . . The script by Stephen Sondheim and Anthony Perkins is a dazzling technical achievement; Herbert Ross's direction is slick, energetic and professional; and most of the performances are first-rate.'

Raquel, for her part, was inclined to try and put the whole affair behind her and flew back to Las Vegas to prepare for her series of live, one-woman shows. She was under no illusions about the task that confronted her as she was to reveal to Peter McDonald in April 1974: 'I was offered the chance to go to Las Vegas and do a show several times and each time I turned it down. I was afraid of failure, I suppose, Las Vegas has been a graveyard for a lot of people who have gone there when their success in films was floundering, and I didn't want that to happen to me. I could imagine all the critics lying in wait with their hatchets. It was my manager who finally persuaded me; he eavesdropped on one of my weekly singing lessons and told me I should do a show.

'The first day we arrived in Las Vegas I remember standing around in my practice leotards, very impatient, saying: "Come on, come on, when is it my turn?" Finally they said: "For God's sake let her on, before she drives us crazy."'

Raquel's reception in Las Vegas was nowhere near as bad as she feared: the critics admired her drive and determination, and the paying public found that there was more to her than just a beautiful face and body.

Although she was still somewhat hurt at the way she had been treated in the press over *The Last of Sheila*, she did not refuse a request for an interview with the top-selling woman's magazine, *Cosmopolitan*. There were, though, traces of bitterness in her words. 'This is a tough business, particularly on women,' she told her interviewer. 'I think I'm tough enough. I hope I am. But they treat you like – like a piece of flesh, a commodity. If you have an idea or suggestion for a script, the director says, "Sure honey, now just shut up and do it like I say." '

While she felt such treatment was degrading, it did not align her with the Female Liberationists who were then gaining a great deal of publicity. 'I'm getting so bored with all that!' she went on vehemently. 'I hate those crusading types, those Joan of Arcs. I hate zealots. Oh, Germaine Greer's all right, and thank God Gloria Steinem is *pretty*! But those others! Jane Fonda and Candy Bergen – I'm so bored reading about what's on their minds! I admire Jane as an actress, but I wouldn't pay attention to anything she has to say. Oh, I am going to get in trouble for saying that! I think the trouble is that women should treat men as sex objects, the way men treat women. It's not such a bad idea, you know!'

In concluding the interview, Raquel also had time for a little soul-searching about her career in general and her lifestyle in particular. 'I'm really going to stop reading what's written about me,' she said. 'With interviewers I don't know, I used to believe the answers I was giving, but then it got so that interviews began to affect me more than I affected them. I started saying things that I felt the interviewers wanted to hear. My main problem, though, is coming back to reality after making a picture. I love sweeping into places, and being fussed over with the make-up and the costumes and the lights. But then I come home, and there's nothing to do.

'Right now I'm redoing my house. I want to make it funkier. I hate to do housework. I hate to cook. My doctor said to me, "You need something to do, for therapy. How about the garden?" I said, "Forget it! I hate gardening." So he said, "How about the house?" So I said, "OK, the house."

'And I'm taking acting lessons. My daughter says, "Mommy, why are you taking acting lessons. You already are an actress." I admit I wasn't really an actress when I started, and a lot of the pictures I made just for the money. But I think I'm getting better.'

Those remarks were to prove a nicely timed piece of optimism, for although her next film, *The Three Musketeers*, was to bring its share of problems, it was also to earn her her first major award as an actress.

The men behind this latest plan to bring Alexander Dumas' evergreen adventure classic to the screen (according to *Variety* it had previously been filmed *thirty-two times* since the first Italian silent version in 1909!) were the Salkind father and son, Alexander and Ilya, who had also produced *Bluebeard*. Their $5 million version was being billed as 'a major swing back to the swashbuckling genre' and by May 1973 a vastly impressive cast had been lined up including Oliver Reed, Frank Finlay and Richard Chamberlain as the musketeers, Michael York (D'Artagnan), Charlton Heston (Cardinal Richelieu), Christopher Lee (Rochfort), Faye Dunaway (Milady), Geraldine Chaplin (Anne of Austria) and Raquel in the delightful role of the heroine, Mme Constance Bonancieux, with the British comedian Spike Milligan, as her miserly, befuddled husband.

Filming of what was intended right from the start to be a slightly off-beat treatment of the story took place around Madrid in Spain, with director Richard Lester who had masterminded The Beatles' hit films, *A Hard Day's Night* and *Help!* The script had been written by George Macdonald Fraser, author of the series of bawdy bestselling novels about the irrepressible letcher, Flashman.

Before shooting began, Ilya Salkind explained that it had originally been planned to make the film in Hungary, 'but we needed twenty-seven different locations and it would have been impossible to cover the distances.' He also revealed that at one time he wanted to cast The Beatles in the picture, then thought of doing a burlesque comedy version with Jerry Lewis and Peter Sellers, but decided it would be dangerous to ridicule the legend. The final cast, he added, had been hand-picked as the best talents available.

Salkind imposed a ban on journalists visiting the locations while shooting was taking place because, he said, three other versions of the story were also being filmed in Europe at the same time and he did not want writers to 'give away secrets that can be stolen for the other pictures'. Naturally, such a policy lead to a proliferation of rumours of accidents and arguments as the summer progressed – a prime example of these being an

English newspaper story that Faye Dunaway and Raquel were not getting along. Mark Shivas of the *New York Times* quashed this particular tale in a dispatch of 5 August. He wrote: 'Faye Dunaway flew in the day before from London, thus putting the lie to an English newspaper story that she and Raquel Welch had already been vying with each other in Madrid for the lowest neckline in the picture, even resorting to their own scissors in a battle of the plunge. "Raquel isn't even due in Spain until September," says Faye, "but we do have a fight scene where we try more or less to tear each other to pieces. Have you seen Dietrich in *Destry Rides Again* in that bar-room brawl? Wild, isn't it? Well, something like that." '

When Raquel did arrive to film her part she decided to put her own ban on interviews, although once again several journalists and writers had converged on Madrid more interested in her than the picture. Almost at once there were stories that she had taken charge of the production and was making demands for changes in the script and in her costumes. (In fact, changes *had* been made to the screenplay since she had first read and accepted the part of Constance, and she *did* want Ron Talsky's expertise as a designer used on her clothes.)

The writer George Feifer who was on hand at the time was somewhat sarcastic about the events, though ultimately objective in his viewpoint. 'Miss Welch's own explanation is that she often arrives at projects to find that scripts have been changed to her detriment,' he wrote. 'She is not consulted, and when the film is released, is made the scapegoat of unfair criticism in terms of "Oh, another Raquel Welch caper". While it is true that many actors arrive on location to find a different script being shot to the one they had read, Miss Welch's demands in this case were sweeping. She insisted on changes in the script. "In short," said an insider to the negotiations, "she got full and final control over everything involving her in the script, even the final cut of the film itself. Can you believe it?" '

But, went on Feifer, 'To blame Raquel Welch for her posture would be as useful as scolding sheiks for pricing their oil according to what the market will endure. As so often, it is the human condition that is at fault: in this case, not merely venal

A superb portrait of Raquel as Mme Bonancieux for her two *Musketeer* roles

producers, but public willingness to buy symbols, sex and other kinds. Miss Welch's rumoured domination of so much of the artistic process enhances my wish to meet her. The publicity man cannot promise an interview. She, as stipulated in her contract, does her own choosing, and will unpredictably agree to see a local reporter, having turned down a formal request from *Time*.'

This interview, the only one which Raquel did give during her stay in Spain as well as being her first to a Spanish journalist, was generally unremarkable although she did make it quite clear to the young female writer that she was well aware of what some people were whispering behind her back. In almost a continuation of her *Cosmopolitan* discussion, she said: 'I'll confess something to you that probably won't surprise you. Raquel Welch is one of the most hated actresses in the film world. You know why? Because I do not tolerate errors or unprofessional behaviour. My hardness is my only weapon. Too many films today show women as stupid beings. There is a lack of good material and a lack of directors. To show the public that I was capable of being an actress, I had to produce my own film.'

The young reporter was evidently very impressed by Raquel and offered a nice description of her from their meeting in the Madrid Hilton: 'Everything about her person is white and luminous. White dress with wide skirts and tight bodice accentuating her tiny figure. Transparent white face surrounded by ringleted hair dressed with pearls. White teeth showing through her luminous smile, competing with the whiteness of her eyes. White, long-fingered and sensitive hands, one of which stretches out to take mine.'

The overwhelming impression given by the article was that despite the intense heat of Spain in September, the gruelling demands of her role, not to mention accidentally spraining her arm in the gutsy scrap with Faye Dunaway which remained in the finished picture – Raquel had not lost her style or her determination, no matter what the gossips said.

Her effort on the film was doubly rewarded. It opened to ecstatic reviews, and in London was premiered at a Royal Command Film Performance attended by the Queen Mother in

March 1974. Virginia Dignam of *The Morning Star* declared the picture to be 'a good cut and thrust above all previous versions . . . altogether a wholly engaging escapade memorable for its sheer abundance and vitality.' And she added: 'Among the lusty men and busty women, Raquel Welch displays a fine comedy sense as the accident-prone go-between, with that lovable eccentric Spike Milligan as her suspicious husband.' Across the Atlantic, Jay Cocks of *Time* also shared the enthusiasm. '*The Three Musketeers* is a surfeit of pleasures,' he wrote. 'It can be said, simply and with thanks, that it is an absolutely terrific movie.' Cocks particularly praised the elements of high humour in the telling of the story and was delighted with the climactic brawl between Raquel and Faye Dunaway.

Off-screen, however, another kind of fight was going on. A rumour that more than enough film had actually been shot in Spain to make not one picture but two, was now revealed to be a fact. *The Three Musketeers* was released with a sub-title, 'The Queen of Diamonds', along with the announcement that the second half of the story was to follow as *The Four Musketeers*, subtitled 'The Revenge of Milady'. *Variety* reported that this announcement had immediately raised a number of questions between the stars and Alexander and Ilya Salkind. 'To the surprise of all,' the newspaper stated on 1 January 1974, 'the completed version of the film includes an overt trailer for a subsequent film, *The Four Musketeers*. The current legal questions relate to whether the latter film represents work performed for a longer film which has been split in two parts; if that be the case, there are a host of compensation queries being drafted.'

By the time the story reached the national newspapers, *The Sun* was speaking in much more dramatic terms. 'Raquel Welch has staged a pay revolt in Hollywood,' the paper declared, 'because she made a film without knowing it. And so did six other stars . . . Oliver Reed, Michael York, Faye Dunaway, Charlton Heston, Richard Chamberlain and Geraldine Chaplin. They were mystified when they saw that the newly released four-hour epic *The Three Musketeers* had been trimmed to only two hours. Then they learned that producer Alexander Salkind planned to use the other two hours for a second film to be called

The Four Musketeers. The Indignant Seven promptly demanded payment for the second film.'

Ten days later, however, the matter had been resolved, the *Evening Standard* reporting a settlement after 'some legal sparring worthy of the best swashbuckling sequences in the picture'. The decision to release two films had been taken after the filming was complete, and a spokesman for the producers was quoted: 'Originally one film was made, lasting four hours. Since it is largely for children and the intermission made a natural break, we decided to release it as two films. Some of the cast were upset but the whole matter is now resolved.'

Again, *The Four Musketeers* got a good public reception, though the critics were generally less satisfied. The *Daily Express* reported that the picture 'has all the ingredients that made its predecessor so successful except one – a high level of comic invention.' It seems, the paper added, 'that Dick Lester used up just about all the Musketeer jokes he could muster in the earlier film.' John Coleman of the *New Statesman* thought the film 'looked perfectly splendid' and while he 'hugely enjoyed the off-screen mutterings, Goon-fashion, to the main action' was nevertheless 'alarmed to find such presences as Raquel Welch being done to death when a joke had been anticipated.' Derek Malcolm of *The Guardian* showed equal sympathy for Raquel declaring, 'Poor Miss Welch, done in most cruelly at the end of the film and battered about unmercifully beforehand, is less well served by it.' All the critics were, though, agreed that her performance proved once and for all that she had a real flair for comedy – Penelope Gilliatt, the doyen of film writers, declaring: 'Mme Bonancieux, as the Queen's dressmaker, carrying perfidious love messages between the sovereign's lady and the enemy Prime Minister of England, is played very funnily by Raquel Welch.'

These accolades were then underlined in a most positive form. For at the annual Golden Globe Awards given for contributions to the performing arts, she was overwhelmingly voted the Year's Best Actress in a Comedy or Musical for her part as Constance Bonancieux. It was a moment of triumph she could justifiably savour – and she did so, saying shortly afterwards:

A moment of high comedy from *The Three Musketeers* (1973)

Raquel with another of her co-stars from the *Musketeer* films, Michael York, meets the Queen Mother at the Royal Film Performance in March 1974

'It's hard to explain just how much it means to me, that award. It means acceptance, for one thing. There it is, proof that somewhere along the line I did something that people enjoyed. I can look at it and think: *That proves it.* Unless you've been put forward as a sex symbol yourself it's hard to explain just what a drag that finally becomes. At first it's terrific. You go along with it. But when you want to grow out of it, you find you can't. That's been the reason for so many of my battles on films – I wanted people to realise I could actually act.'

Perhaps more than anything else, the award put Raquel in great heart for the next picture on her schedule. A picture which was to result in what many people believe to be her finest screen performance to date.

9 A Very Special Party

BEFORE BEGINNING WORK on what has since proved to be a major achievement in her film career, *The Wild Party*, Raquel made a television special for CBS, in April 1974, which realised the dream she had nurtured ever since she saw Frank Sinatra perform in Miami. For a whole hour she dominated the screen in *Really Raquel*, dancing, singing and making jokes. She was only accompanied by one male dancer and some puppets.

The basis of the programme was her one-woman show which she had painstakingly perfected before the demanding audiences of Las Vegas, and now she bowled over the nation's TV viewers as well as the small screen critics. 'The sex symbol has broadened out into an all-round entertainer,' declared the *Los Angeles Times*. 'A triumph against all the odds,' added *Variety*.

The stunning costumes which Raquel wore in the show had been specially designed by Ron Talsky, who was also the executive producer. He said he had placed great emphasis on making her look soft and feminine and added, 'I see a great gentleness in her'. Friends who knew the couple also thought that Raquel was becoming mellower and happier, and she herself said of their relationship: 'Ours is the kind of love that survives various ups and downs – the fights and insecurities and the bad times when you're feeling terrible and the bad things that happen from the outside. I really want to try to be successful with a relationship that can go through such highs and lows. It's a real challenge.' Talsky's support and enthusiasm behind the scenes was undoubtedly an important factor in the success of *Really Raquel*.

Apart from dazzling her audience with her dancing, Raquel sang with style and again utilised her talent for comedy – several times having fun at her own expense. After her first two songs she paused to smile at her audience and comment, 'Well, I guess you didn't think I'd get this far!'

Later, sitting on a stool, she recited what she called 'the myths about that other Raquel – the public one'. One myth is that she is actually a man. 'Next time you read or hear something about me,' she said, 'I hope you'll remember this little piece of advice.' And with that she broke into the song, 'It Ain't Necessarily So'.

In one of her finest roles, as Queenie, in *The Wild Party* (1975)

157

After the performance Raquel talked to the press about her reasons for making the show. 'Everything I did in it,' she said, 'I had wanted to do for years, and had never been given the chance. When I went into films I had a completely false idea of what they would be like. I wanted it to be like old Fred Astaire and Ginger Rogers films, lots of marvellous music, witty dialogue and dancing. Of course, I came into films at quite the wrong time for all that, so I did the best I could – I tried to play all these over-heroic ladies and sensual nymphs for comedy because I couldn't take them seriously. I think I survived all the rubbish – I hope I did anyway.'

Because of the success of the show, Raquel also hoped it would be shown outside America, 'so that people will realise that I have a bit more to recommend me than the size of my bust.' Her wish was fulfilled almost immediately in Britain where the programme went out as *Show of the Week* on BBC in the last week of April. Talking to Peter McDonald of the *Radio Times*, Raquel said: 'I feel that doing this show has let me out of a cage that I have been in for too long. I'd love to do another television show, something a little less elegant, more darn dirty – *really* Raquel!'

Once again her words anticipated the next phase of her career, playing a sluttish beauty in *The Wild Party*. It was also something of a strange quirk of fate that she should have been going into this particular film. She had once been the hit of the night at one of Hollywood's most lavish parties at which guests were invited to dress up as their favourite film stars. Raquel, being expert at doing her own make-up, decided to turn herself into one of her screen idols, Katharine Hepburn, whom she had actually never met. So she pinned up her hair in the casual Hepburn style, topped it with a floppy Hepburn hat, and wore a pair of baggy slacks, sneakers and an army field jacket. The finished disguise – complete with Hepburn freckles, high cheek-bones, the down-curled mouth with pouty lips and almost Oriental eyes – was an astonishingly close facsimile of the original. At the party she was stopped by almost every guest. 'I know who you are – you're Katharine Hepburn,' she was challenged. 'But *who* are you really?' At this, Raquel would push out her chest, put her hands on her hips and grin, 'Would you believe Raquel Welch?'

The men behind the making of the film *The Wild Party* were James Ivory and Ismail Merchant, a director/producer team who had made their names with a string of popular films from India including *Shakespeare Wallah* and *The Householder*, and more recently with the highly-acclaimed *Heat and Dust*. The basis of the picture was the real-life scandal at a Labour Day Party in 1920 when the silent comedy film star, Fatty Arbuckle, made sexual approaches to a young starlet, Virginia Rappe, that were so violent, or else so clumsy, that they resulted in the girl's death. Although the manslaughter charges against Arbuckle were finally dropped (and the exact nature of the girl's injuries never made public), his career never recovered and he died a virtually forgotten man in 1932. These facts, plus a long satirical poem called *The Wild Party*, written by Joseph Moncure March in 1928, which also focused on show business decadence in the twenties, were utilised by the scriptwriter, Walter Marks, in what became a powerful and evocative study of the underside of Hollywood.

Filming of the picture took place in April and May at the Mission Inn at Riverside, California, a hotel used by many famous stars in the twenties and also occasionally employed for sneak previews of new pictures. The fact that its pirate-ship-like interiors complete with Chinese lanterns had survived virtually intact from that period made it the perfect background for the story.

Cast in the 'Fatty Arbuckle' role under the name of Jolly Grimm was the accomplished character actor, James Coco, with Raquel as his mistress, Queenie, and Perry King as a narcissistic movie swashbuckler called Dale Sword. The film describes the lavish party which Grimm throws to celebrate his new picture which he hopes will bring to a halt his rapid decline as a star.

Talking about the actual filming of the picture, Ismail Merchant said afterwards: 'Right from the very first day *The Wild Party* started, we all lived in Howard Johnson's. We had everybody, from the production boy to Raquel Welch, all staying together. There wasn't this special treatment, special chairs written with their names, Raquel Welch, Jimmy Coco, The Director, and all that. We didn't have any of that paraphernalia. We all worked for the same movie with the same devotion and the same feeling. We're all stars! The production boy is a star in my film and Raquel Welch is a star. There are no distinctions and I don't want to make distinctions, because that is how they make those hollow, shallow films.'

Merchant's partner, James Ivory, also revealed how they had come to pick Raquel for her role as Queenie:'We were having great trouble finding someone for the film,' he said. 'She had to play a kind of corrupt, beautiful ex-chorus girl, mistress of a fading movie star. And we just couldn't find a girl that was right. We weren't looking for a big star necessarily. Then I saw the *Today Show* and Raquel was on. She seemed very intelligent, and interesting, and she said she'd like to do comedy and she wanted to play different roles than she'd been playing, so we sent her the script.'

Ivory found his hunch about Raquel paid immediate dividends. 'The truth of the matter,' he said, 'is that Raquel's very, very good. There are some things she's done, some shots we've taken, scenes we've done, which I like as much as anything that we've ever done in any of our films. There are one or two long monologue scenes she does which are terribly good, I think, and she's never been seen like this in any film, but when we were doing them I could not tell her or convince her that they were good. In fact, that was true of the whole film.'

Ismail Merchant also added his own comment on Raquel. 'You know,' he said, 'when you talk about Raquel Welch, people take it as a joke! People take it as a joke in the sense of this sexy symbol, where she's being described as a woman with a pair of boobs and that's all there is of her, so a walk-on part would be enough for her. Like a ten-minute session in a film is enough. You see Raquel Welch and you have all your kicks. But here, it's a different thing. There was some kind of an honesty that came across, and Jim felt it and said that, yes, Queenie would have this kind of electrifying pull . . . Raquel certainly does have that star quality, there's no doubt about that. That's why she's a star, I guess. I mean, it's not for nothing that someone becomes a star.'

Raquel, for her part, threw herself into the role with great enthusiasm and though she may have had doubts that her work was as good as James Ivory claimed, was quick to report that she thought the picture was being made in a serious way and 'has some beautiful film in it'. She also found working with James Coco a very rewarding experience.

'I loved working with Jimmy Coco,' she told Andy Warhol the following December, 'because I just think he's so sensational. He's such a wonderful actor. And the thing that I love is that we got this relationship working in the film that was really terrific. Because Perry King is playing the handsome guy in the film and the normal trend of a part like that would be to throw over the less-obvious character of a heavy-set silent-screen comedian who looks like Jimmy Coco, for the dashing young hero Dale Sword – that's the obvious thing.

'But I was interested in building up the relationship between Coco and the girl. Because I felt that that was real and the other thing was not. And I enjoy doing that very much. Because he would have been a father-figure to her, and that's the kind of person that she would gravitate to – rather than to a handsome somebody who would be a roll in the hay. Those kinds of things are not that difficult to come by – it's those other nurturing qualities that are attractive.'

It was a tragedy, then, that after all this care and effort had been expended on *The Wild Party*, the financiers, American International Pictures, had it re-edited immediately it was complete. James Ivory was naturally furious at what he considered the ruination of his musical, which he believed to be expressionist, very stylised and lyrical.

'A GIRL CALLED QUEENIE'

In discussing his picture, director James Ivory said, 'The moods of *The Wild Party* are based on the various moods or various stages of the party as it is described in the Joseph Moncure March poem. Indeed, the whole structure of the film is based on that of the poem.' This is how the author describes Queenie, the character played by Raquel:

> Queenie was a blonde, and her age stood still,
> And she danced twice a day in vaudeville.
> Grey eyes.
> Lips like coals aglow.
> Her face was a tinted mask of snow.
> What hips—
> What shoulders—
> What a back she had!
> Her legs were built to drive men mad.
> And she did.
> She would skid.
> But sooner or later they bored her:
> Sixteen a year was her order.
>
> They might be blackguards;
> They might be curs;
> They might be actors; sports; chauffeurs—
> She never inquired
> Of the men she desired
> About their social status, or wealth;
> She was only concerned about their health.
> True:
> She knew:
> There was little she hadn't been through.
> And she liked her lovers violent, and vicious:
> Queenie was sexually ambitious.
> So:
> Now you know.
> A fascinating woman, as they go.

'They did more than re-edit it,' he told the *Daily Express*'s
Ron Benson. 'They butchered it. Scenes were cut out, discarded, sex scenes were put in. It was a cheap attempt to over-
exploit the exploitable. It was a mess.'

Perhaps not surprisingly the picture was badly received by
the American critics when it opened in August and did not fare
well at the box-office. *Time* called it a 'strange movie . . . which
never develops the fine frenzy it needs.' For once, though, the
magazine rushed to Raquel's defence: 'Welch's presence is
usually the occasion for unchivalrous wisecracks of one sort or
another, but she is genuinely touching in *The Wild Party*. Her
Queenie is a really sensual woman, not a creature of synthetic
sexuality. Unhappily, *The Wild Party* may be the first of her
starring vehicles in which she is actually better than the material.'

Things went from bad to worse when the picture crossed the
Atlantic to open in London. The British Censor ordered three
more minutes of cuts in the film before it could be released.
James Ivory now found that out of sixty scenes in the picture,
only three remained completely intact – and they were musical
numbers. 'I was beside myself,' Ivory recalled later. 'It was the
worst episode of my life. I pleaded with American International
Pictures but to no avail.'

Rather than let the English critics savage *The Wild Party* even
more than their American counterparts had done, Ivory wrote to
each of them explaining what had happened to the picture since
he had finished shooting.

'The wreck that is about to be released in London as my
work is not just a shortened, souped-up *Wild Party*,' he wrote, 'it
is the distributor's cheap attempt to over-exploit everything
exploitable, with discarded sex scenes piled on top of the ones I
had already included: with poor scenes that were dropped by me
in the editing room stuck back in the hope of some easy laughs
. . . with flashbacks and flashforwards thrust into the middle of
perfectly workable scenes and so forth. All the dialogue scenes
have either been very much shortened or eliminated entirely.
Most foolish of all, the distributor, afraid that Jolly Grimm was
not coming across as a 'lovable' character, has tried to make him
more so by cutting important scenes of Coco that had a bite in

them, which has the further curious effect on the picture of throwing Raquel Welch's performance off centre.

'The whole thing is a mess now, and though I can't disassociate myself from it entirely, and don't really like to – I do want to call your attention to what has happened to my film,' James Ivory concluded.

David Robinson of *The Times* took Ivory's point and felt it would be 'impertinent to discuss a film in such a version', but did believe there were 'some remnants of a promising idea remaining' as well as 'something to admire in Raquel Welch's anguished performance as Queenie'.

Kenneth Robinson of *The Spectator* admitted he saw the picture *before* he read James Ivory's letter. 'Whatever the distributors have done to the production,' he decided, 'the poetry persists and I have a feeling James Ivory made a better picture than he knew. Even after its adulteration it has the quality of a modern morality play.'

Nigel Andrews of the *Financial Times* could not agree, however, declaring: 'At no time do the film's talented parts look like adding up to an effective whole. The finished product, though full of promising details and images that linger in the mind, ends up an exotic failure for which much of the blame must lie at the door of the film's distributors, American International Pictures.

'I would doubt that the authorised version of *The Wild Party* is quite the masterpiece that its status as a *cause célèbre* helps to suggest. But there can be no doubt that American International have made things worse; and that what might at least have been a critical success for Ivory, if no great shakes at the box-office, is now doomed to sink without trace in both areas.'

Such indeed might have been the case had James Ivory not continued to believe in his work and then in July 1980 finally persuaded BBC Television to show his original work in its entirety. And so, *The Wild Party* which ends up on the screen in death and scandal had a happy ending at last. (It was also subsequently re-released for cinema showing in 1982.) 'This really is my version,' an ecstatic Ivory told the press on 12 July 1980. 'It is a poetic, artistic work. It is good, I like it very much. It restores some of my faith.'

The critics, too, now gave unstinting praise to *The Wild Party*, and all singled out Raquel's unadulterated performance as the best of her career. A particular highlight was considered the reinstatement of the sequence in which she sung her 'naughty' song, *Singapore Sally*. 'This uncut version amply confirms that Raquel Welch never gave a better performance,' wrote Derek Malcolm in *The Guardian*, while Felix Barker in the *Evening News* applauded, 'With her wide, lip-sticked mouth turned down at the corners, Miss Welch has the bad-tempered look of a spoilt, self-indulgent slut and she plays the part to perfection.' And Margaret Hinxman, the doyen of the *Daily Mail*, judged simply, 'Raquel Welch's sad, glamorous Queenie is quite the most confident acting she has ever done.'

Aside from demonstrating emphatically how good an actress Raquel could be when someone gave her a real chance, *The Wild Party* also started something of a vogue in pictures about the seamier side of Hollywood life and history, with photo-biographies of W. C. Fields, Carole Lombard, Clark Gable, Marilyn Monroe and Joan Crawford all following in quick succession.

This ultimate acclaim for Raquel's performance was, of course, still in the future in 1974, but there were other consolations for her. *Variety* declared she was now the sixth most bankable star in Hollywood and able to pick and choose her parts at will. This also enabled her to spend time at home with her two rapidly growing-up children, Damon (15) and Tahnee (13). As well, she found time to be chairwoman of the 1975 American Cancer Crusade, a cause dear to her heart.

She was, though, deeply hurt when at a press conference in New York, a journalist suggested her image was too frivolous for such a position. She burst into tears and sobbed, 'I think that's very cruel.' Just how vulnerable she could still feel despite all the acclaim came out in an interview she gave to Roderick Mann in February 1975. 'You wouldn't believe some of the things I've had to put up with in my career,' she said. 'Even when you finally break away from the sex symbol thing and get a chance to show you can do some acting, people keep watching you. It's rather like being an ex-convict. They keep waiting for you to

Raquel displays her marvellous
talent for impersonation as
Katharine Hepburn at a
Hollywood party

make a slip and wind up back where you started from. People are really spiteful and cruel. Anyway, from now on I am going to do more and more films for my own company.'

Raquel also revealed to Mann that she and Ron Talsky had separated. 'My relationship with Ron was the best I've ever had in my life,' she said. 'We've broken up now, but we're still good friends.' A proud, independent man, Ron had decided he did not want to be an appendage to Raquel's career, tagging around from movie set to television studio and nightclub stage. Despite the split, though, they were to remain in touch and met from time to time for dinner.

On the eternal question of her striking good looks and the confidence that they *should* give her to face anything, Raquel told Roderick Mann: 'Confidence has to come from inside, right? And I have never really liked the way I look. I mean, I'd have given anything to look like Julie Christie. Or Candice Bergen. Well' – a small smile – 'almost anything. I think they're both so attractive. If I had my choice I would have Candice's face on my body. I would keep my own body.'

The equally enduring question of her body came up in another interview at this time – with Timothy Ferris of the influential *Rolling Stone* magazine. Raquel was both outspoken and angry in her responses. 'Look,' she said, 'I know I'm supposed to be silicone from the knees up; my ass has been lifted; I've had a rib removed; my teeth are not my own, and so on. Actresses call me up and ask, "Who did your tits?" Well, I've never had any such surgery. It's so irritating when they say I have. What can I do? Sue? Give everybody a squeeze test? I mean, fuck it. The truth is I've had nothing done. I wouldn't lie to you. I was given good equipment in the beginning and I've looked after it, that's all. I would be terrified of surgery.'

Raquel went on equally vehemently. 'A lot has been made over the gigantic dimensions of my breasts,' she said. 'It's total myth. I'm really a rather normal-sized lady of good proportions and a nice figure. I have a tiny waist and I go in and out and I'm not that voluptuous, as you can see.

'People sit and wait for me to turn them on. I think to myself, what the hell, why should I come on to some guy? I can see he's not interested in *me*. It's not *me* he's especially interested in. It's Raquel Welch! The label. He's after the label.

'To have it said that you're a sex symbol, the most beautiful girl in the world, is initially terrific. You think, isn't that neat? Then you pass a mirror and you say, "Uh-oh, that face ain't gonna launch a thousand ships, and that bod's not so hot either." Nobody can be the most beautiful girl in the world. It's just fairytale time. There was a huge discrepancy between the symbol – Raquel Welch – and what I could ever aspire to be for real. The stupidity of it is that once somebody says you're something, you try to *be* it. That's the stupidity.

'Now, after some psychotherapy, I've come to grips with the monster and said OK, there's the public thing, the label. It means money and the chance to do other things. It's going to be tough, but using it you can open up the other side and let people find out you're a serious artist.'

As a representative of *the* pioneer magazine in the discussion of drugs, it was only natural that Timothy Ferris raised the subject with Raquel. 'I've never been into a drug culture or felt that I was a head or anything,' she told him. 'I *was* intrigued from time to time for a while about what it was that was making everybody more – *aware*. But I myself would never toy with any of what I think of as hard drugs, and that includes coke. I have never taken coke and hope I never do. I have smoked dope and I probably will continue to. But I'm not interested in getting into anything harder. My kids know I smoke and they're not very happy about it. I think their generation is more conservative.'

Perhaps, though, the most interesting item of all in the *Rolling Stone* interview was a short postscript which Raquel wrote herself and forwarded to Timothy Ferris. It came perhaps closer to revealing the complex character of this remarkable woman than any of her quotes, and certainly much of it remains as true today as when it was written. The message is handwritten on yellow paper and begins: 'Dear Tim'.

'I cannot lose the feeling,' she begins, 'that I haven't communicated all I wanted to, to you. It's not that I didn't talk – God knows I can rap – but maybe I expected to come up with some answers for myself. I don't ask myself those metaphysical questions you did – about why I am the way I am, whether I'm happy, secure, etc. Well, not verbally, only subconsciously. I thought I should write these words to you. I mean, I did the interview to say something, and I ended up not saying it.

'I am really fed up doing second-rate roles in mediocre films and working against the prejudice that comes with my "image". I have studied all my life. I am not trying to *become* an actress, I *am* an artist and an actress. An actor's life is the only place there is for me to practise and stretch the muscles of my craft, which otherwise I haven't had the chance to use.

'I'm now planning to devote more time to areas outside my career in films, away from the vicious Hollywood gossip that hammers home until it is reflex action for people to think of me as a silicone Barbie Doll. I am going to develop some film properties I own and devote time to the theatre and to the music field. I'd like to cut an album with my favourite musicians, for example J. J. Cale, Randy Newman, the Jazz Crusaders hopefully!, and perhaps go on tour as a singer with a big band. I'm just discovering myself musically and I really dig it. It's the best.

'The film industry and even my agents do not get the picture about me. They don't think I care about my craft. To the greater public I'm the American walking, talking Coke bottle, the Marlboro woman. I hate it. I laugh 'cause it's funny, but I hate it. Let's face it, how do you live the life of a Coke bottle? There's no tangibility to my "image". I doubt if people even believe my parts move. Well, they do, they do.

'I would work for practically nothing to do a film by Truffaut or Schlesinger, George Roy Hill, Billy Friedkin . . . You see, it's not a question of fame, money, success; it's a question of living and *doing* something I want to do well.

'Also – last plea to cop – I'm not a phenomenon who exists out of time, an anachronism of sociological significance. I'm a person.'

This page was signed: 'Love, Raquel'. It was a moving testament from a woman who at last seemed to have come to terms with herself *and* knew where she was going.

Raquel with co-star James Coco in the attempted rape scene from *The Wild Party*

10 The Last Hollywood Sex Symbol

AFTER THE DRAMA of *The Wild Party* – both on screen and off – Raquel went to something much lighter and funnier for her next picture, the jokily titled *Mother, Jugs and Speed*. It provided another chance to demonstrate her talent for comedy as well as playing the kind of 'sexy dame' that delighted her worldwide audiences.

The story concerned the activities of a group of ambulance drivers in Los Angeles where independent rival companies compete with one another to collect the victims of drugs, drink, suicide, unrequited love, childbirth and violence of one kind or another. The three central figures of the story, Orlin 'Mother' Tucker (played by the black comedian Bill Cosby), Jennifer 'Jugs' Jurgens (Raquel) and Tony 'Speed' Malatesta (Harvey Keitel) work for the F & B Ambulance Service in frantic competition with the Unity Ambulance Company to deliver paying patients to hospital. Their nicknames, which give the film its title, are derived from their characteristics: Cosby from the negro term of abuse, Harvey Keitel for his skill as a driver and Raquel – as one reviewer was to put it with rather more taste than the rest – 'from her forthcoming attractions'.

There was much about *Mother, Jugs and Speed* to remind audiences of the enormously successful television series *M*A*S*H*, and scriptwriter Tom Mankiewicz gave the story much of the same frenetic energy and black comedy. He managed to portray the dark underside of a big city like Los Angeles with a mixture of tragedy and satire, showing how the sick can be exploited by the ruthless 'pay first, die later' system which exists in America. The British director, Peter Yates, fresh from his triumph with *Bullit*, encouraged fine performances from his cast, particularly Raquel, who 'loved every minute' of making the picture.

Though *Newsweek* magazine had reservations about the film in its June 1976 review, there was praise for Raquel's performance. 'In the movie she does not like to be called "Jugs",' said the journal, 'and the sympathies of the film-makers are entirely with her, even as they exploit her. But Welch retains a vestige of dignity and a little something more. As last year's *The Wild Party* demonstrated, Welch can handle an emotionally

173

diverse role. She has a moment here mourning the death of a pregnant mother in which she is quite affecting – although director Peter Yates has edited the scene much to her advantage. Still, she is agile and relaxed, and does not seem particularly out of place either up against the effortless cool of Bill Cosby or the brush-fire intensity of Harvey Keitel, who is among the best young actors around.'

In Britain, Arthur Thirkell of the *Daily Mirror* found the picture 'often painfully funny' while Virginia Dignam of the *Morning Star* again complimented Raquel on her acting, in particular for her delivery of a 'would-be feminist statement'. Surprisingly, no one noticed another performance by a man destined to become the most famous 'villain-you-love-to-hate' of the 1980s, Larry Hagman – the notorious 'J.R.' of the television soap opera *Dallas*.

Because she had always wanted to be more than just a movie actress – and with the recent successes of the television spectacular *Really Raquel* and the film *The Wild Party* still fresh in people's minds – Raquel decided now to spend more time on the third area of her career, live entertainment. She had proved that unlike most Hollywood stars she could appear on television as well as film, and now wanted to secure her reputation on the stage.

To achieve this objective she set herself the kind of demanding schedule of performances that would have made even the most hardened and experienced live pro entertainer blanch. Beginning in August 1975 in Cincinnati, she gave a total of ninety-eight concerts in eighty-six days in a dozen different cities. Accompanying her on the tour were an entourage of seventeen musicians and three dancers, as well as her personal assistants. The song and dance extravaganza included two dance routines, an extract from a rock ballet, some comedy sketches and eight songs.

Raquel had never underestimated the enormity of the task she had set herself: nor was she unprepared for setbacks. At her very first concert in Cincinnati she had to cope with almost constant barracking from a member of the audience who kept shouting 'Get them off!' But the public's initial wariness was overcome by the sheer vitality and determination of her performance.

'If you are an artist you like to use all your talent,' she explained during the course of the tour. 'I've always thought I had a real talent for musical comedy . . . but when I tried to sell the idea of a Raquel Welch musical, people laughed. I thought, ''I'll show 'em.'' '

And show them she did. It cost her $100,000 to put together what she called her 'singin', dancin', wisecrackin' one-woman show'. And a lot more in terms of sweat and pain. Her opening performances were not overly successful, she admits, and she had to make urgent changes. She took extra singing lessons *over the phone* from her coach in New York, and rehearsed her dance sequences until her feet bled. Such was her determination to give her all that she actually knocked herself out on a piece of scenery when leaving the stage during one performance and only came to just in time to change for her next act.

But it was all worthwhile when she was hailed as a 'real trouper' and played to packed houses as her tour progressed across America, through Europe and finally to South America.

Two interesting encounters awaited her at the end of the tour in Rio, a place she came to like. 'It's very easy to be sensuous there,' she says. 'All those sexy beach boys gazing at me with their big eyes.' First, she met the former American Secretary of State, Henry Kissinger. During the course of their animated conversation about their respective interests in politics and show business, Kissinger asked her, 'Tell me, Raquel, what does an ex-Secretary of State do?' To which Raquel replied with typical wit, 'I have the same problem, Henry. What does an ex-sex symbol do?'

Her second encounter was with a handsome young Brazilian, Paulo Pilla, a musicians' manager. 'It was during carnival time,' she said later. 'He asked me to go out dancing. But I was tired, as usual. So I said no. Then I realised that if I didn't go I might never see him again. So I went. Then he asked me to dance. Again I said no. Then I realised that if I didn't, I might never get a chance to be close to him. So we danced. And that was that.

'At that time there was a 'flu epidemic in Brazil. One paper called it the Paulo Pilla 'flu because – "It strikes suddenly and knocks you off your feet." But it could equally have been called the Raquel Welch 'flu. It goes away and then comes right back. For that's what I did. I went to Canada to do a show and then flew right back to Paulo.'

Raquel was delighted when her children, Damon and Tahnee, took to Paulo and he was soon seen increasingly at her side. 'He's very special,' she said, 'and come to think of it, that may be my life from now on – traipsing round the world after Paulo.'

In fact, it turned out to be quite the opposite and it was Paulo who followed Raquel when in August she set off for Europe once again to be reunited with the father and son partnership of Alexander and Ilya Salkind on another new picture based on a classic story, *The Prince and the Pauper* by Mark Twain.

The familiar story had been brought to the screen five times previously, from a silent version in 1909 to Walt Disney's 1962 production directed by Don Chaffey. Young Prince Edward, the son of Henry VIII, and the beggar boy, Tom Canty, look exactly alike and accidentally change places. Their separate adventures in the royal courts and mean streets of the country ensue before they are dramatically reinstated in their true positions at the coronation of the new King. The Salkinds' $9 million wide-screen version was filmed partly in England (at Penhurst Palace near Tonbridge in Kent, and in Pinewood Studios) with the major sections being shot on the banks of the Danube around Budapest and the medieval village of Sopron.

As in the case of both *Bluebeard* and the two Musketeer films, the Salkinds loaded the picture with star names, reuniting Raquel (playing Edith) with Oliver Reed (as Miles Hendon, the soldier of fortune who with Edith befriends the wandering Prince) and Charlton Heston as Henry VIII. Mark Lester (of *Oliver* fame) played the dual role of the Prince and the Pauper; David Hemmings as Hugh Hendon, Miles' brother; Ernest Borgnine as the wicked John Canty, the beggar boy's father; George C. Scott as the evil Ruffler; and Rex Harrison and Harry Andrews as two noblemen, Norfolk and Hertford.

176

With the talented Harvey Keitel in *Mother, Jugs and Speed* (1976)

Once again – just as had occurred on previous occasions – the reporters from no fewer than seven countries who were invited to visit the Hungarian locations were more anxious to see Raquel than any of the other stars. 'Many of them,' *Variety* reported on 25 August, 'came only at the prospect of pinning down Raquel Welch for a "full confession" interview.' She, though, was obviously much happier than during her stay in sweltering Spain and this time made herself fully available 'answering all questions coolly, but never evasively', according to the film trade newspaper.

Much of the familiar ground about her 'synthetic beauty' and her alleged difficulty to work with were covered with remorseless persistence, though Roderick Mann who took her to dinner at the charming Alabardos Restaurant overlooking the

A moment of private grief:
Raquel reading messages at
the funeral of her father in
May 1976

Danube, found himself compelled to remark in the face of all the wisecracks of his colleagues: 'She is looking spectacular. Because she is that coelacanth of showbusiness – the last surviving Hollywood sex symbol – the fact that she is a beautiful woman is often overlooked.'

Raquel wanted the chance to clear up an idea that had been gaining ground that she and Oliver Reed had fallen out. Rumours had persisted since their time together in Spain that they disliked each other intensely. 'I must say he's been quite charming,' she told the pressmen. 'When I arrived here I said, "You know, I'm very vulnerable." And he said, "Don't worry, so am I." After that everything was fine.'

She said the pair of them had even had a little lighthearted fun at the expense of their so-called feud. 'After a couple of drinks we staged a mock shouting match at each other. You should have seen the look of alarm on the face of the producer, Pierre Spengler. He thought his worst fears were being realised!'

She was well aware that certain people spoke badly of her – 'because there is a lot of animosity in this business'.

'You know,' she said, 'when people meet me they usually change their minds about me. But I can't meet everyone. Do you know when my English hairdresser told friends she was coming to work with me they told her: "That old bitch surrounds herself with a lot of trolls. She can't bear to have beautiful women anywhere near." Isn't that an incredible thing to say about someone you don't even know? I know I'm supposed to be a sex symbol, but the truth is I'm not a terribly sexy person. Not unless I'm emotionally involved with a man. Then it's different. So I suppose I disappoint a lot of people when they meet me. They've read about this great sex symbol and they expect extraordinary things of me. But what can I do? I mean, I can't just stand there undulating, can I?'

Standing still was certainly not something Raquel was prepared to do as she threw herself into more concert work and television appearances as soon as her role in *The Prince and the Pauper* was complete. A casualty of all this activity, though, was her romance with Paulo Pilla. 'Enough was enough,' said Raquel later in the year. 'I'm happy we are no longer involved.'

She was quite prepared to admit that the publicity which followed her everywhere and the label of being 'Raquel Welch's boyfriend' which was hung around Paulo's neck had not helped their relationship. Nor had the travelling. 'I've had only a week off in the past year,' she said. 'I don't know how my romance with Paulo lasted six months. Well, really, if you counted all the time we spent together it would only amount to about six weeks. You see, any man I'm involved with has to do a lot of travelling. I lead such a strange life, moving from movie locations to night-clubs and concerts. It isn't easy to have a relationship.'

Paulo was, in fact, soon forgotten in work, and a particularly enjoyable engagement came in December when she guested on a television special hosted by Country and Western singer Mac Davis. She did a musical number with twenty children which delighted the audience.

'The whole concept of the show had to do with children and Christmas,' she said afterwards. 'I had a wonderful time doing it. I like to do television work because it keeps the public up to date with what I'm doing. I do quite different things in pictures than I do on TV. Performers in Europe think the same way that I do on this subject. Besides, there are many people watching television who never go to the movies. And some moviegoers refuse to watch television. And there's a completely different audience in nightclubs and concert halls. I want to reach as many of them as possible. Television viewers see what I'm like as a personality,' she went on, 'and relate directly with Raquel Welch. In movies I'm playing a character, not myself. It's fun playing a character as I do in *The Prince and the Pauper* or a sexy dame fighting off the boys in *Mother, Jugs and Speed*, which I did before that. But neither one has much to do with me as a person.'

Raquel said that she felt her versatility as an entertainer would help her break away from the sex goddess image. But just making movies she would only be offered the same kind of cliché roles that had made her a star.

While talking to the press she also revealed that she had bought the screen rights to a Japanese novel, *Woman of the Dunes* by Kobo Abe, which she was hoping to film in Mexico with the

Raquel was reunited again with Oliver Reed to star in *The Prince and the Pauper* (1976) with Mark Lester as the central character

leading French director, Louis Malle.

What was quite settled now was that she was handling all her own affairs. 'I'm too independent to have anyone deciding what I do now,' she said. 'I make my own decisions. When a night-club date, a television show or a movie is brought to me, I'm asked how I feel about it, not *told* that I'm going to do it. I refuse to be pushed by anyone or forced into a situation I don't like or know is wrong for me.'

Her decision to diversify could not have been more emphatically vindicated than when *The Prince and the Pauper* opened in the spring of 1977 and was almost universally condemned. In America, where it was retitled *Crossed Swords*, the picture was savaged by Frank Rich of *Time* who said, 'The real issue raised by this film is why it was made at all. There just isn't much of a market for a movie like this in the US any more; family films are too slow for adults and too tame for children raised on ABC sitcoms and *Star Wars*.' Rich had little good to say about the cast whom he called a 'mishmash', although he did concede: 'Even the wretched performances – Mark Lester's prissy portrayal of the title roles aside – are fun in their bizarre way. Ernest Borgnine yells out his lines in an unabashed American accent and bulges his eyes in every close-up, proving once again that he is the last word in screen vulgarity. His crass pyrotechnics are almost topped by Charlton Heston, who turns Henry VIII's death scene into a veritable anthology of hammy acting gestures. Raquel Welch, no fool, sees to it that she is more seen than heard.'

The picture fared no better in Britain where it retained its original title. 'Tudor tosh,' Tom Hutchinson of the *Sunday Telegraph* called it and went on: 'A tale of great entertaining historical melodrama has been made paltry. Stunning sets and illuminating stars have been trivialised. It is a film that should be ashamed of itself.' Russell Davies of the *Observer* was equally unimpressed calling the picture 'a gaudy ruin, populated by actorial rogues looking out on the world with varying degrees of seriousness.' And caught up in the general lunacy of all the reviews he added: 'Collectors of Great Entrances will want to see Raquel Welch's here. Materialising at the top of some cardboard stairs, she gives the bosoms the Big Flex, just to reassure us they're still there. I enjoyed this.'

Only the veteran reviewer Patrick Gibbs of the *Daily Telegraph* could bring himself almost begrudgingly to find something to praise. 'Raquel Welch's talents are wasted,' he said, 'indeed invisible, as a lady of virtue, and only Oliver Reed as the soldier of fortune comes out of the ordeal really well.'

Raquel could certainly not have enjoyed reading these reviews, and despite the euphoria of the stage and television work, she was feeling a growing sense of restlessness, as she told Nancy Anderson: 'I don't seem to know what success is any more,' she said. 'I think many people are given drive by the delusion that, if they reach certain professional plateaux in movies or music or whatever, they will automatically be at peace with themselves and all the bad things in life will go away. But it doesn't happen like that. You reach the plateau, and the unhappiness is still there. You look around and say, ''Hey, wait a minute! I'm supposed to have everything. I can show it to you in black and white. There it is. It says I'm this and that and the other. I'm the person who has it all.'' However, I'm not happy. What went wrong?'

Worry, Raquel thought, seemed to be one of her major problems. 'I wish I could break the habit of worrying,' she went on. 'I've gotten away from it a lot during the past few years, because I've had to look back at my past, and when I do that, I realise that all the worrying I used to do was pointless. It didn't accomplish anything. Everything turned out fine, and the worrying didn't help. But just give me anything, and I tend to worry about it. I'll worry about my work. I'll worry about the scene that's coming up. I'll worry about the way I look; about what I'm wearing; about the house not being painted. I used to worry about what I'd do when I quit making pictures and wonder what could ever possibly be as wonderful and exciting and as great as what I'm doing today. Now, though, I don't worry about that so much, because I think I could just sit and do nothing very well. Well, actually, not just nothing. I'd like a beautiful home and be able to entertain my friends and meet interesting people.'

Raquel with co-star Jean-Paul
Belmondo making *The Animal*
in Paris in 1978

11 The French Connection

IN HER REVEALING interview with Nancy Anderson, Raquel had spoken eloquently about her restless creative drive and her need for 'new things, new inspirations'. And that is precisely what she set out to find in the spring of 1977 when she left for Paris to make a film entirely in French!

She had always been a girl with more guts and determination than most people give her credit for. But this was a particularly gutsy thing to do, for she agreed to co-star with the leading French actor Jean-Paul Belmondo in *L'Animal*, a picture to be made in a language she only spoke hesitantly. When asked about her decision, she was disarmingly frank. 'I suppose it did take a lot of guts,' she said, 'but it was one of the best things I ever did because that's where I met André. He was a friend of the director. And when you've started out in a film like *One Million Years BC*, you've got to be prepared to take chances like that.'

Before Raquel left Los Angeles, she took French classes at the Berlitz Institute, but this still left her unprepared for what happened in the Paris studios. 'For the first two weeks I was literally terrified,' she said. 'Everyone talked to me at sixty miles an hour and I couldn't understand a word of what was being said. But gradually I got used to it. Jean-Paul Belmondo was marvellous. He made me feel – as the French say – *fantasmer*. After all, he is very attractive. And since I appeal to men, there is surely no reason why certain men should not appeal to me in the same way? Even though I had learned certain phrases so that we could be polite to one another, we still didn't understand each other all the time, though we got on very well. I am very fond of him.'

Raquel also got on well with her director Claude Zizi, who called her performance 'verrree good', and co-stars Danny Saval, Raymond Gérôme and Charles Gérard.

L'Animal told the story of an out-of-work stunt man (Belmondo) who quarrels with his girlfriend (Raquel) and throws both of them into a series of comic situations when he is unwittingly mistaken for an effeminate and rather cowardly actor who is almost identical to him in appearance. Raquel adapted well to the stylish ways of French comedy acting, and was provided with some excellent dialogue by scriptwriter Michael Audiard. Belmondo, now nearly fifty, enjoyed the dual role of stunt man and the actor, as well as 'rewarding himself' – as one French magazine put it – 'for twenty years of success with a co-starring role with the Hollywood sex symbol, Raquel Welch.'

Paris Match decided that Belmondo was 'terrific – but with such trump cards as Miss Welch and such a budget it would be difficult to be otherwise.' And *Telerama* declared simply, 'The story is terrific – he has talent, this animal, and Raquel Welch who is *so* pretty!'

Somebody else who met Raquel off the set during the making of *L'Animal* thought she was very pretty, too. One evening she was invited to dinner at a restaurant by Claude Zizi, and among the guests was a young, rather sombre-looking French writer and film producer named André Weinfeld. André, then aged thirty-three, was almost struck dumb to find himself in the company of the legendary American sex symbol. 'I was intimidated at finding Raquel at the same table and I behaved rather arrogantly,' he said later, 'which is my way of dealing with shyness.'

Raquel, though, was not aware of any arrogance on the young man's part – in fact she was captivated by him. She also revealed afterwards how close they had been to *not* meeting at all. 'He was dragged out of his sick bed to come and have dinner with me,' she said, 'because the director was a little intimidated by me and didn't know what to say. I thought André was charming and utterly fascinating and felt that he had a very historic face – a mixture of Mick Jagger and Don Quixote. André was also very gentlemanly. He didn't come on strong like most men might. He just kissed me goodnight at my door and left me.'

The next day André said he felt a little guilty for his behaviour at dinner – unaware of the impact he had made – and sent a bunch of orchids and asked if he might take her to dinner. Raquel accepted, but brought two friends as chaperones. However, as she now remembers with a smile, they were sent home before the dessert course was reached.

It was love at first sight. 'I felt I saw everything in that one face that I could possibly want,' Raquel said, 'humour, intelligence, sensuality. André is such a terrific person that sometimes it hurts. I think to myself, ''God, what was life like before him, what would it be without him?'' I think he is spectacular!'

André, for his part, says that the first thing that impressed him about Raquel was not her beauty. 'It was her humour – her humour about everything. About the world. About herself. I was just not *expecting* it. I also hadn't expected her intelligence, or the originality of her mind, either. But what really made me fall in love with her was that I found her to be very vulnerable. It struck a chord in my French heart.'

Raquel finished *L'Animal* almost in a dream. The couple sent each other loving messages every day and they took to spending their evenings wandering around Paris. Only once were they followed by a man. Unable to shake him off, Raquel ducked into a toilet in a restaurant. Still he followed her and, confronting her, begged to be allowed to paint her.

'What?' she exclaimed. 'Here?'

Although Raquel and André went to holiday in Sardinia immediately after filming was complete, news of their romance had already reached the press. 'The story of the romance between Raquel Welch and André Weinfeld reads like something from a film script,' the *Daily Mirror* wrote. 'Beautiful Hollywood sex symbol meets penniless French writer, they fall in love and live happily ever after.' And the reporter added, 'I hope for their sake that's how it works out.'

Raquel was aware from past experience how the press's constant interest in her could jeopardise their relationship. 'I am trying to protect him,' she said in July of that same year, 'for it is terrible to see someone you love being devoured by publicity. It happened with Paulo Pilla. Being the boyfriend of Raquel Welch made life very difficult for him. I felt as if I had stolen his identity. I shall do everything I can to prevent that happening to André.'

Overleaf: An early picture with André Weinfeld, now Raquel's third husband

The meeting of André with Raquel's teenage son and daughter who came to France on holiday, was not easy, either. 'We spent a weekend together at a little cottage,' she said.

'André was charming to them, but the children came near to killing him. Of course, it was jealousy and entirely understandable. But kids can be horrible. Obviously they know that any man who loves me will certainly butter them up. Their attitude is one of ''I'm her daughter, and I'm her son. So what?'' That was really very difficult for André.'

Raquel could also see that life was not easy for Damon and Tahnee either. Her daughter was always being told how much like her mother she was – a remark she hated. While Damon suffered from realising that all his friends were in love with his mother.

'In some ways my children are very privileged,' she said. 'I used to wonder where they were going to find any adversity to push them in a direction. But I think life supplies those things for us. Now my kids are reacting against a whole different set of things. I'm the tough act to follow, and they don't want to follow. It's harder for them to have a personal sense of identity, harder for them to find a direction because they've always had material things. I've tried not to spoil them, but they still live in a big house in Beverly Hills. Their mother's still Raquel Welch. So to the other young people they know, they may look like they've really got it all: they're beautiful, bright, charming. They live in a great house. Their mother is famous. Isn't it terrific? But I don't see them as having the world on a string. I see the kids grappling with life just like I did.'

The family problems were soon overcome, however, and André moved to Beverly Hills to be with Raquel. The only cloud on their horizon was the occasional sniping of the Hollywood gossip columnists, and the delight of some of them nicknaming them 'Beauty and the Beast'. While André would certainly not describe himself as handsome, he has the French quality of *joli-laia* which many people find more attractive. Raquel being foremost among these.

During the next two years the couple were inseparable, travelling between Raquel's house in California, André's in Paris, and finding a joint apartment in New York. Aside from his own commitments as a scriptwriter and producer, André took an increasing interest in Raquel's work and career and naturally enough soon became her most trusted adviser.

It was, therefore, the most natural thing in the world when the couple got married on 5 July 1980. Raquel, just two months from her fortieth birthday and a woman who had seemed hesitant about the idea of a third marriage after the failure of her first two, was now in no doubt that André was the special man she had been looking for. She even gave him an affectionate nickname 'Poupougne', and told the press, 'He may not be the most handsome creature in the world, but I love him because he is himself: he's relaxed and he's extremely funny.'

By a strange quirk of fate, shortly before Raquel met André in 1977, she saw her first husband, Jim Welch, again for the first time since their separation fifteen years earlier. Although Patrick Curtis had legally adopted Raquel's two children Welch had always been anxious to try and keep an eye on their progress. Their meeting was a traumatic one, as Raquel explained shortly after.

'Jim just telephoned me one day to say he would like to come to see his children,' she said. 'I was so nervous I changed my dress a dozen times while I was waiting for him. It was stupid to get into such a state, I know, but you must realise that I hadn't seen him for a very long time. And he was my first love and the father of my children.

'He was very well and I could see that he was prospering. He said I looked well, too, and he was pleased at my success. For the rest of the time we talked about the children and their future. We hardly mentioned the past at all.'

With André by her side, time passed happily for Raquel as she continued with her television work and concert and night-club appearances. All were enormously successful, and when certain people expressed surprise at this success, she replied with considerable dignity, 'But somebody is always being surprised about me. I suppose because expectations are so low as far as I'm concerned that almost anything is a surprise. Most people don't think I can even finish a sentence.'

In November 1978 she returned to England, where her fame had first begun, to make a guest appearance on the most popular television programme of the moment, *The Muppet Show*. Her arrival was fanfared with headlines and the press followed her every move looking for stories. A London taxi driver reported how Raquel refused to kiss her date in the back seat of his cab, and the story made headlines the next morning. 'Fortunately I had the good sense to laugh about that,' she says. 'That kind of thing is just a giggle. It's vaguely annoying, but there have been other things so much nastier and much more upsetting. People who set out to be venomous. It's really upsetting to think there's that much negative energy coming in your direction, that someone will sit down, with all that venom inside them, and just pour it all over you.'

Such was the interest in her, that when Raquel arrived at the television studios at Elstree to work on *The Muppet Show* she found the place crowded with spectators. Everyone, it seemed, wanted to watch the superstar at work – but Raquel was understandably having none of it.

'I'm perfectly happy to be looked at when I'm at a premiere or the Academy Awards,' she said, 'or doing my nightclub act where people come to see me wear sparkly dresses. But when I'm working I get so preoccupied I can't stand it. It makes me nervous. At that moment I don't want to be reminded that I'm an oddity. For, you know, movie people are only an extension of what circuses used to be. I'm a target for a lot of things. Any taxi driver, milkman, secretary, hairdresser, manicurist, anybody who wants to say something about me can say it . . . and have done.'

With the distractions out of the way, Raquel quickly demonstrated her absolute professionalism when it came to her work. She knew her lines perfectly and launched herself into her songs, dance routines and even improvised dialogue for her delightful numbers with the 'stars' of the show, Kermit the frog, the inimitable Miss Piggy, and Fozzy Bear.

Journalist Byron Rogers admiring Raquel's professionalism wrote: 'Four floors above the council houses and the graffiti of Boreham Wood, the sex symbol of her time stood making eyes at three feet of carpet material held on a man's hand. The song had been her idea. "Confide in me/Rely on me/And I will try/and satisfy/your every need." She stroked the carpet material as she sang. She played with its little brown hat. Bending down to it, she told it that it was sexy. In turn the puppet on the hand of a bald, bespectacled American became bashful, thrilled, then overcome by its own importance. All this was cut short when Raquel Welch suggested he might like to come up to her room. Fozzy Bear collapsed. ''Can I . . . bring a friend?'' '

During her visit to Britain, Raquel revealed that during the past eighteen months she had turned down all the movie scripts which had been offered to her while she was working on ideas of her own. 'I have made almost thirty films and spent two-thirds of my career surviving mediocre material,' she said. 'If I appear in crap there is no way I can survive other than on my looks. And that has got to be a bore. Being photogenic and being received as a beautiful woman is terrific, but if I am going to go on playing in movies, the stories and the characters have got to work. I don't care if I play a heroin addict or a bikini-clad jet-setter as long as it is a story that will touch people. I don't have to do the other kind of stuff any more. I have had enough fame. I have enough money. All the dreams I had as a child have come true.'

In fact, she said, the idea that most excited her was a film with her own daughter, Tahnee, now sixteen years old. 'The idea is to investigate the relationship between a mother and daughter,' she said, 'and what it means at this age when women have become more professional and financially independent. At this point in my life I feel like the best thing I could do for myself is what authors do – draw on their own experiences. Most of mine, fortunately, have not been exposed because I've not offered up my private life to the world. I think I've been fairly circumspect. This film will be based on another side of me that most people have never seen.

'I don't have any illusions about myself as a great sainted mother,' she went on. 'I think I've been a very good mother. But I don't for a minute delude myself that I work for any other reason than I want to be in the public eye and I am not going to let anything keep me from it.'

Raquel said she saw herself as a combination of mother and career woman and hoped that the projected film would put

André with Raquel and her two children, Tahnee and Damon

across her view that a woman didn't have to make a choice between one or the other. 'Somewhere between the feminist and the girlie magazines is the woman who has tried to have the best of all the things that were offered to her,' she continued. 'I don't think that's been totally captured by the media yet, especially the idea of the woman who enjoys being a mother. Too many women feel motherhood is unrewarding.

'I'm glad I didn't make that decision to be alone. I'm glad I didn't feel children would upset the scheme of things. Now, if someone with an image like mine made a statement in favour of motherhood – that might change a lot of people's minds. Women say: "Oh, having babies will destroy my figure." They think: "I won't be desirable any more. Men won't be interested in me. I'll be just a burden to them."

'This film will give me a chance to express things that are very close to me. It will be a meaty dramatic role, and will also be very funny.'

Sadly, Raquel has not so far turned this compelling idea into reality, although instead she did go into a perhaps equally challenging role the following year when she played the part of an Indian squaw who during the course of the story changes from a young girl to an aged grandmother. Before beginning work, though, she had some important news for the press.

'I'm too old to be a sex symbol,' she announced in February 1979 – and promptly grabbed the world's headlines.

'After thirteen years as a top glamour queen Raquel Welch is to abdicate,' wrote Thomson Prentice in the *Daily Mail*. 'The world's leading female fantasy figure has decided: "Thirty-eight is too old to be a sex symbol."'

Raquel's statement said, 'I must accept the fact that I am beginning to get old. I'm certainly not going to welcome the sight of a lot of wrinkles. Ageing can be harder on a woman who has relied on her looks as I have most of my life. But at last I have started using my head rather than my body. It's time for someone younger to take over. I used to think the best thing in the world was being a sex object. I still think it's wonderful in its way. But I am going to do pictures that do not focus just on the flesh between my ankles and my neck. I used to get the feeling that women just looked at me for the stitch marks, and yet it is 100 per cent untrue that I have had either a facelift or a silicone job. I'm just lucky to be so naturally good-looking.'

And she added: 'It is very difficult to be a sex symbol. People pick on you. They don't want to believe you're any good – that would make you even more of a threat.'

It was an explosive announcement – although there were very few people who believed Raquel was in serious danger of losing her public appeal.

Curiously, too, something almost literally explosive occurred when, after a series of appearances in America, Raquel flew back to London in April to make a television spectacular with her friend, Bob Hope, at the London Palladium.

Because of the enjoyment she had had when making the special trip to Vietnam to perform for American troops with the veteran entertainer, Raquel had been delighted to accept Hope's invitation to appear on the show. For a week she rehearsed her number in which she played a chorus girl who is 'discovered' by Bob Hope, playing an old-time Broadway producer.

Then, on the day of the television recording, the Palladium was suddenly thrown into chaos. There had been a threat that a bomb had been planted in the famous old theatre. Raquel, who had been all through such an emergency before when making *The Last of Sheila*, calmly left the stage while the building was combed by police and bomb squad officers. When, later, the all-clear was given, she returned to work as calmly as if nothing had happened. No one who later watched the spectacular on television would have suspected what proceeded the highlight of Raquel's scene with Bob Hope when he picks her from a line of chorus girls and says he will star her in his show *Follies of 1927*.

'But,' says Raquel, 'it's only 1923.'

'I like long rehearsals,' Hope grinned.

An incident such as that with the bomb scare might have been enough to age anyone – but for Raquel that particular experience took place when she left London shortly afterwards and flew to the little town of Billings, Montana, to make a two-and-a-half-hour long television epic, *The Legend of Walks Far Woman*. In this she played an Indian squaw of mixed Sioux and

Blackfoot blood whose life is traced from the 1870s until just after World War II. It was her television début in a movie drama.

The story had been adapted by the bestselling novelist Evan Hunter from a book by Colin Stuart. In a preface to the book it is stated that *Walks Far Woman* was 'drawn in part from the memories of two Montana women the author knew in his boyhood'.

Walks Far Woman is a nineteenth century Indian squaw who becomes caught up in the maelstrom that was Montana in the era of the battle of the Little Big Horn. She is a fiercely independent woman, though, and she rejects prospective husbands, saves the life of a drowning chief, enters a foot race and breaks a bucking bronco. She also marries, gives birth, sees her infant daughter die, loots dead cavalry troopers, stabs her husband and witnesses the demise of the free roaming ways of the Sioux – all as she progresses indestructably to the age of ninety.

The picture was beyond any doubt the most dramatic and physically demanding she had ever undertaken. The actual filming took six weeks and for most days Raquel worked up to fourteen hours, often in temperatures of 90 degrees. Understandably, tempers sometimes frayed in these conditions, and there were arguments, though many of the press stories of feuding and fighting were typically over-sensational.

Raquel was enthusiasm and determination personified right from the start. Though she injured her knee on one occasion and had to go to hospital to be treated for food poisoning on another, nothing would deter her. 'I really wanted to sufficiently immerse myself in a character so that people wouldn't see me as Raquel Welch any more,' she said afterwards. 'That is to say the Raquel Welch they see on the Academy Awards presentations. It was important for me to do that, and I think I succeeded. In a sense the picture is an Indian version of *Jane Pittman*. I think that was part of its appeal to me. I like the idea of heroines who survive and struggle. It's important to have your own principles, to have dignity and follow your own code, as Walks Far does. I like a woman character with backbone.'

Raquel also explained that she had long been interested in

the American Indians, partly because her father was Bolivian and she had 'some Indian blood in her veins'. And she added, 'We tried to be accurate in our portrayal of Indian life. We wanted to show the strong influence of custom and tribal life. At the same time, we tried not to be over-reverent about it. We didn't want it to be the old noble-savage portrayal. If the film has a message, then the most important thing it can say is that these people are human beings and they have the same foibles we have.'

Raquel could well understand that some people might have been sceptical of her in a role such as *Walks Far Woman* because 'it's, well, a change of pace', she said. 'With all my other characters, their problems were usually psychological. But this role was completely different. This woman is fighting for survival, fleeing from her old tribe and trying to set up a new existence.

'I'm not ashamed of my earlier work and I didn't play Walks Far as a closet exercise. I wanted people to see it and enjoy it and – if it's not too pretentious to say – to learn from it. As Sam Goldwyn said, "Never preach".'

When, yet again, there were stories about alleged troubles in making the picture all Raquel would say was, 'That is the price you sometimes have to pay for getting something well done.'

The American critics, however, did not like the film. One or two condemned the picture as 'so bad it is funny', while others felt it was a disaster, saved only by Raquel's 'remarkable performance'. John J. O'Connor of the *New York Times* found himself somewhere between two camps. 'There is nothing dreadfully wrong with Miss Welch's performance,' he wrote, 'although her flowing hair and dazzling teeth do tend to get in the way of verisimilitude in depictions of everyday Indian life in Montana territory starting in the mid-1870s. It's just that the entire story is boring as it trudges through clichés about Indian nobility and the stupid ways of the white man . . .'

Across the Atlantic, however, *The Legend of Walks Far Woman* came in for more favourable comment. Nina Hibbin, of the *New Statesman*, having just seen a revival of the 1939 John Wayne classic, *Stagecoach*, drew an interesting conclusion by comparing the two pictures. '*Walks Far Woman*,' she said, 'was filmed for TV in 1979. It portrays the Sioux as lively individuals showing a highly-developed sense of fair play and communal living. Made forty years earlier, *Stagecoach*, which opened BBC-2's season of John Ford films, represents the Indians as brutal and mindless savages. In terms of visual imagery, pace and narrative style, *Stagecoach* knocks spots off *Walks Far Woman*. But in human terms it's the other way round. The TV time-warp has a worrying capacity for undermining the progress of ideas and perpetuating the sins of the past.'

And of Raquel's performance from girl to old woman, she added, 'She's very effective, as it happens, and although her presence adds to the film's romantic gloss, it doesn't detract from its clear-cut pro-Indian sympathies.'

If Raquel was in any way deterred by the critics' lack of enthusiasm for the film, she did not show it publicly – or waver in her determination to accept only the roles of real worth. She proved this most emphatically in March 1980 when she told the press she had turned down a fee of *one million dollars* to appear naked and do a rape scene in a forthcoming film, *The Fan Club*. 'What they wanted me to do made me sick and shocked,' she said. 'They wanted me to play a rape scene. Now to be raped itself is an emotional and tragic experience – but to be raped before the movie cameras is just awful. I have never used my body for explicit sex scenes, and the nude ones in this movie really scared me. The producers raised the fee to try to get me to do it, but I said a firm no. There's too much sex and violence on the screens anyhow.'

In complete contrast to this suggested film, Raquel decided on making another television special with André helping her as co-writer and producer. As the couple had been married in July it would be their first joint venture as husband and wife. And as it would be screened just after her fortieth birthday, Raquel decided to use it as an opportunity to have a little fun with her own career and image.

Called *From Raquel With Love*, the show presented her as a cliché-kind of glamour girl seeking fame and fortune in New York. In endeavouring to get herself a flat in a very respectable

Rehearsing with David Frost
for the Bob Hope Show in
London, April 1979

area she had to dress in a very straitlaced manner – but somehow the pose went wrong. Parts of the show were almost a direct
playback of Raquel's life – except that here she played them for
laughs. Her heroine was a sexy beauty who looked as if she
would have the world at her fingertips at any moment – but
something was always going wrong.

'It was my way of making fun of the whole sex symbol
business,' she said. 'I managed to poke some fun at glamour
girls. It was about time. Let me tell you something about being a
glamour girl. It's a damned difficult role to play. Once you do it
as well as Marilyn Monroe did, you have to try and carry it on.
It's terribly hard to create, even for a moment, the illusion of
being a sex symbol. It's almost impossible to sustain. And it
certainly isn't the sum total of what I am able to do.'

The year 1980 *should* have ended on a high note for Raquel.
There had been the television breakthrough in *The Legend of
Walks Far Woman*, the record-breaking success of her live
appearances, and what she hoped was freedom at last from her
tag as a Sex Goddess. Instead, in a few horrendous weeks,
everything seemed to go wrong.

First there had been a series of highly unflattering newspaper
'revelations' from her former hairdresser and confidante, Mary
Bredin, who accused Raquel of being thoughtless and mean,
said she wasn't really sexy at all and wanted to retire at forty 'so
nobody could see her faded looks'.

Then came more 'inside stories' from her former secretary,
Sheldon Hughes, who said that although she was always
immaculately made-up and dressed when in public, at home she
spent most of her time in a white towelling robe or men's
pyjamas. He also claimed she had a terrible temper, would let
fly four letter words, and could be pernickety about the smallest
things. 'Beauty, wealth and fame are hers in abundance,' said
Hughes, 'but insecurity and jealousy lurk beneath the surface.'

He claimed that Raquel was trying to put a brave face on
reaching forty. 'But she is frightened of growing old,' he went
on. 'She still regards her body as her biggest asset. Shedding the
sex symbol image isn't going to be that easy for her.' What
Hughes could not deny, though, was that she had preserved her

looks very well. 'She has an excellent body and works hard at dieting and yoga to keep it in shape,' he added.

Raquel, not surprisingly, dismissed both sets of revelations. 'The only way to deal with garbage like that is to take it between the tips of your fingers and drop it into the toilet. Those people are real parasites: they write crap to make money off somebody else's reputation. And people like me are very vulnerable to that sort of exploitation.'

The third blow was the hardest of all to bear. As the year drew to a close she began work on what she hoped would be her next dramatic role – a part in the MGM film of John Steinbeck's classic novel of depression times in California, *Cannery Row*.

Then, with the world in the throes of enjoying Christmas, a terse announcement from MGM said that Raquel had been dropped from the picture after only four days' work. She was to be replaced by Debra Winger, the girl who had played opposite John Travolta in *Urban Cowboy*.

'I've never been so hurt or shocked,' Raquel told enquiring newsmen as she flew home. 'I don't know why it has happened. No one complained to me about anything. I'm completely flattened. The damage this has done my career is too horrible to think about.' As the new year began, she was almost on the verge of tears as she told friends, 'This is the lowest point of my career.'

If only she had known that it was, in fact, to be a prelude to her greatest triumph and the final transition from sex symbol to a superstar on top of the world of entertainment . . .

12 Woman of the Year

SUCH WAS RAQUEL'S distress at being sacked from the cast of *Cannery Row* in December 1980 that she met with her lawyer, George Slaff, in the new year and decided to sue MGM for a massive $24,578,888. After filing the suit in Los Angeles Superior Court on 10 February, she told pressmen that she was seeking punitive damages for unfair dismissal and loss of professional standing. She claimed that the studio had used her name to recruit other stars for the picture but as a result of her dismissal, 'I am now out of work because I turned down other film offers to make *Cannery Row*. I have no idea when I will work again,' she added.

The details of Raquel's suit against MGM are worth examining because she felt that apart from her personal loss, the dismissal raised some important issues with regard to studio-actor relationships in general. Speaking after the suit had been lodged, Raquel said: 'I am determined to prove through this suit that the "removal" of myself as an actress from *Cannery Row* by MGM constitutes a blatant and premeditated breach of contract on their part. They have also tried to hold my professional conduct up to speculation and ridicule, thereby making me the scapegoat for their own faults.'

Raquel accused the studio of breach-of-contract, conspiracy, slander and infliction of emotional distress, in addition to not paying her money due under an alleged pay-or-play contract. She claimed that the defendants 'made various false statements that Raquel Welch had failed to perform obligations required by her and that she had refused reasonable requests made by the producer,' adding that such allegedly false statements caused her 'great damage'. She added that she was 'always on the set, made-up, well before the time of her call' and that the defendants had conspired to spread word she had failed to perform her obligations.

The crux of the matter, as Raquel saw it, lay in the implications her sacking had for the industry as a whole, and she concluded her suit: 'Hopefully this action will have some meaningful effect in drawing attention to the increasing trend in our movie-making industry to characterise creative artists as capricious and undisciplined, thus casting blame on them for the

Raquel receives a Golden Globe Award in Hollywood

shortcomings and lack of knowledge so blatant among some studio hierarchy and some so-called producers today, most of whom stand idly by unable to aid or abet production difficulties, simply because they haven't the slightest idea of the ''how to'' part of film-making.'

Having filed the suit, there was nothing more that Raquel could do, for the wheels of the law grind just as slowly in America as elsewhere.* The whole business of *Cannery Row* had left her dejected and, as she had said, feeling that her career was at its nadir.

As many another writer has observed, Hollywood can be the most friendly place in the world when you're on top. But become involved in a legal wrangle with the hierarchy and it's the loneliest place on earth. Although Raquel's circle of close friends were quick to offer words of sympathy and support, she could not deny the awful chill of apprehension she felt. What did the future hold? *Had* she any future to look forward to?

'After *Cannery Row* I thought I was completely dead,' she said later. 'It stunned me. I never want to feel that way again – I'd rather die for real.'

At least Raquel had André to console her. And the guts to go on despite the odds. She had not been beaten before and, as the weeks passed, the resolution not to be beaten *this* time grew in her. Perhaps a change of scenery would be good, Raquel thought – away from Hollywood she might have a chance to erase the memory of that bleak day on the Montana location.

'There wasn't a lot to be encouraged about just then,' she said, 'which is why André and I were thinking about moving to New York permanently. He didn't like Hollywood much in any case, and so we began house-hunting in Connecticut. Then, out of the blue, I got this phone call from New York.'

---

* The *New York Times* reported the latest development in this continuing legal wrangle on 12 July 1982. 'Raquel Welch has lost a legal battle in California,' the paper stated. 'Judge Arthur Baldonado of the Superior Court rejected her request for an immediate payment of $400,000 to make up for earnings she lost after being dismissed from the cast of the film *Cannery Row*. In a suit against MGM, in which she said her professional reputation had been damaged, Miss Welch had also sought $2 million in general damages. Her lawyer, George Slaff, said he would appeal the ruling.'

That phone call was to change her life. But to accept the challenge it offered, required the biggest display of determination and courage Raquel had ever been asked to show. 'The call was from the producers of the Broadway show, *Woman of the Year*. They wanted to know if I'd be interested in taking over from the star, Lauren Bacall, when she went on vacation for two weeks in December,' she said.

Raquel held her breath. She was being offered a marvellous opportunity in a musical play which had proved one of the hits of Broadway. If she succeeded, it would re-establish her overnight. If not . . .

She made up her mind. She asked to read the script and said she would fly to New York to see the play. The events of the next few months are vividly etched in her mind. 'When I first got the script, I remember sitting up in bed one night reading it,' she said. 'There's this one lyric in which the character sings, "I'm right, I'm perfectly right. It's remarkably rare that I'm wrong." I turned to my husband, and I said, "André, listen to this. This woman is a perfect bitch. Do you think I can play her?" And he said, "Darling, you'll be wonderful."'

It was the first really good laugh the couple had enjoyed in months, and so Raquel decided to go and see the play at first hand. At the Palace Theatre she found herself instantly captivated. 'I found it fun and fast moving, and watching it I knew I could play it in a different way to Lauren Bacall, so there'd be no question of imitating her. Still, I knew I'd be sticking my neck out. I called Bob Fosse, the film director, who'd always encouraged me since he had seen me do cabaret. "Should I try it?" I asked, "or will they kill me?" "They won't kill you if you're good," he said. "So make sure you have plenty of time to rehearse."

'But,' she added, 'most people weren't that encouraging. "Don't do it," they advised. Even the night before I opened someone said, "Why are you doing it?"'

Raquel had, in fact, already decided for herself why she was doing the play. As she admitted to Glen Collins in May 1982: 'If it hadn't been for the *Cannery Row* experience, I probably wouldn't have been predisposed to stick my neck out on *Woman of the Year*. Why? Because I could have been creamed by the New York critics. But I knew I could cut it, the singing and dancing. I've been doing that all my life. But there's something about Raquel Welch setting foot for the first time on a Broadway stage. Originally, I think the producers thought it would be a cute idea to put me up there for two weeks. But it was a big gamble. I could have bombed.'

As Raquel said earlier, she was determined *not* to be a carbon copy of the woman she was standing in for. 'I may have had more guts than brains to try to follow Bacall,' she admits now, 'but I was not stupid enough to try to copy her. When I saw her do it, I thought she was wonderful. But I saw there were other ways to play it without changing a word. Doing the show was in no way a sure thing for me, but I had to try.'

Before she took over the role of the tough but shapely journalist, Tessa Harding, in the musical which had been based on the 1942 film of the same name starring Spencer Tracy and Katharine Hepburn, she took Bob Fosse's advice and rehearsed like crazy. Although she had nothing to prove when it came to singing and dancing as a result of her years of experience on concert stages and in television, she spent hours working with director Robert Moore and her co-star Jamie Ross. Photographs of her in leotard and thigh-length leg-warmers going through her routines which found their way into American newspapers fascinated as well as intrigued readers. What on earth was the sex goddess (retired) trying now?

Raquel prepared herself exhaustively for a month, losing at least ten pounds in the process. 'I just had to,' she said, 'I mean the Palace was the theatre where Katharine Hepburn, Claudette Colbert, Lena Horne and Lauren Bacall had all appeared, and I couldn't just go on because I wanted to. I remember on the evening of my first performance I could hardly enter my dressing-room just thinking of all the ''greats'' who had been there before. But inside I found on the mirror a little note ''Good Luck. Enjoy yourself. Tessa.'' Tessa is, of course, the heroine of the play but it was actually from Lauren Bacall.

'I was also terrified of the New York critics, of course. I thought they'd tear me down just because I made my name as a glamour girl. So I just kept my mind on the audience and decided that they were the people who really mattered,' she added.

Raquel's performance that night – and on the remaining thirteen evenings – was a triumph. Her hard work, her dedication, her *talent* swept all before her. The New York critics who had actually bought their own tickets and, according to the rumours, had come ready to sneer, stayed instead to cheer.

The *New York Times*, never given to overstatement, rhapsodised, 'When was the last time you heard wolf whistles in a Broadway theatre?' and the doyen of the critics, the usually acerbic Clive Barnes, enthused in the *New York Post*, 'A terrific musical comedy'. Douglas Watt in the *Daily News* hit the nail clean on the head when he wrote, 'Broadway's ready for Raquel Welch and she's ready for Broadway.'

Though she had left the stage to a thunderous ovation and numerous curtain calls, Raquel still waited anxiously for the reviews. 'When we got the papers,' she recalled later, 'the only way I can describe it is the phrase, "The thrill of a lifetime". They just turned things round for me. It was acceptance as an actress and a performer. An incredible change for me.' And speaking of her actual performance she said, 'I finally got a chance to prove in the flesh what I'd been saying all along – that I'm a better actress than anyone knows. The first minute I stepped out on that stage and people began applauding, I just knew I'd beaten every bad rap that people had hung on me.'

Indeed she had. Before that first night was over Raquel had been asked to return to the musical when Lauren Bacall finished her contract run the following summer. As one journalist remarked later, 'For Miss Welch, at forty-one, it is a time of new beginnings.' Another called it simply 'Miss Welch's new incarnation'. *Life* magazine the following week gave her the much-sought-after accolade of her portrait on the front cover.

There was, naturally, something of a feeling of let-down when she flew back to Los Angeles at the end of her fortnight's run. 'After all that glory in New York I felt just like a junkie coming down from a fix. I knew I just had to go back.'

Although she kept herself busy in the interim, Raquel was

perhaps even more nervous when she returned to New York as the permanent star of *Woman of the Year* in June. 'Suddenly, it was my show,' she said. 'The first time I'd been just a replacement. That's when I'd said, "Even if the critics don't like me they can't close me because I close in two weeks anyway." Now it was quite different.'

Her return was not helped by the fact that Lauren Bacall left the show less than pleased at Raquel's sensational success during her two-week run. She had been responsible for helping the show land four of the much coveted Tony Awards in 1981, but her year and a half stint had become overshadowed in the deluge of publicity which greeted Raquel. She left the star's dressing-room at the Palace Theatre stripped bare without the traditional good luck token awaiting the incoming performer. The newspapers predictably made a meal of this so-called 'feud', the *Daily Mirror* calling the changeover 'about the most anti-social event since the assassination of President Lincoln'.

But even such omens could not deny Raquel her success. She reappeared on the stage in a stunning gold lamé gown to a standing ovation that lasted two minutes. And a critic who had previously shown some reservations about her performance could only gasp, 'She is like a dazzling Christmas tree ornament, full of grace, charm and vibrancy.' Queues were soon running around the block and box-office takings soared. (In one week alone receipts were a record $325,810!)

Outside the Palace Theatre, before and after performances, Raquel found herself beseiged by fans. The *Sunday Express*'s Roderick Mann who saw this crush one night when he took her to dinner observed that her 'eventual exit was worthy of the Broadway Star she has become – looking glamorous and happy, she moved among the crowd, signing autographs and accepting compliments. She's now New York's Golden Girl.' Philip Finn of the sister paper, the *Daily Express*, marvelled at the way Raquel was now 'stepping through town with all the panache one expects from a Broadway Queen . . . she has become a success in the show because she made sure she did things her own way.'

Rarely had truer words been spoken about her. And close

friends were quick to observe that her triumph had given her a confidence that twenty years of film-making had scarcely been able to do. The accolades for her performance were genuinely unstinted: rarely had that happened before. She herself was quick to appreciate the amazing change in her life that the play had brought.

'I didn't realise I craved success until I found it in *Woman of the Year*,' she told Toni Miller. 'I suppose I was so used to people regarding me as a sex object that I guess I didn't give it any real thought. Although, deep down, I wanted to prove my talent as a serious actress. Thanks to this play I have been given a legitimacy as an actress, simply because it's the theatre and we all tend to think that's the nitty gritty as far as proving you're good.

'It's one up for me that I managed to pull it off. There have been very few actresses who have done that, particularly my kind of actress, the more glam, sexy Hollywood type.'

As the weeks passed and the demand for tickets for *Woman of the Year* made it become increasingly obvious that Raquel would be asked to extend her initial six months' contract further, there were signs of other changes in her fortunes. 'Since I've been with the show that dark cloud which hung over me after *Cannery Row* seems to have disappeared,' she said in November 1982. 'Suddenly I'm getting calls from people in Hollywood I respect, all because I've made it on Broadway. And now all those people who felt they had a right to treat me shabbily in Hollywood have lost that licence. I've won my stripes. Everyone knows you can't go out and do eight shows a week and get the kind of grosses we're making and not be a professional. I've gone from just being a sex symbol to being thought of as a legitimate actress. And about time too!' she added.

When Raquel passed her forty-second birthday in September, still giving her all on Broadway, there was increasing interest in how she managed to maintain both her stamina and her looks. That she was as beautiful as ever – perhaps even more so – was undeniable and highlighted by the front cover pictures she was given by such prestigious magazines as the American *Playboy Fashion*, British *Cosmopolitan* and French *Paris Match*. The secret, she revealed, was good health, brought about by discipline and hard work.

'I do take care of myself,' she said, 'because health is extremely important, once that goes you have nothing. I don't eat salt, sugar or oil. I eat boiled fish, grilled meat and steamed vegetables. Yes, it takes a lot of self-discipline to do it, as it does making figure eights with my legs early in the morning. Yoga is wonderful and helps me a lot. I spend at least an hour a day at it, mainly Hatha, or physical Yoga, with the breathing exercises. I find it gives me more energy and stamina, and makes me more relaxed and patient as well. I don't smoke or drink because they age the tissues. I used to think people would find me square because I don't drink. It used to embarrass me, but the fact of the matter is my body cannot take it. I'm perfectly happy being in the company of people who drink, though.'

Raquel is by no means a slimming fanatic, nor does she go in for a rigorous diet regimen, for she does enjoy a real slap-up feed now and then: an entire chocolate cake or a French loaf with butter and strawberry jam, being among her favourites. She also thinks it is important to 'think beautiful' as a prescription to staying beautiful. She believes that it is easier for people in show business to afford the luxury and expense of looking great, 'yet every woman can learn how to do it if she has the ambition and the discipline,' she says.

Perhaps not surprisingly in the light of her well considered ideas on health, Raquel was contracted not long afterwards to write a book giving her tips on beauty, dieting and how to develop a personal style. She plans to illustrate the work, due in 1984, with photographs of herself in various Yoga positions. (As an indication of the prospective publisher's faith in her appeal as a writer, they agreed to pay her an advance of £169,000 for the book!)

At this time Raquel also told a writer from *Cine Revue* that apart from watching her health, she had a list of 'Recipes for Success' which she had been following for the past fifteen years. The most important she listed as being: Having faith in each undertaking. Refusing to pose in the nude. Revealing the sexy side of one's personality by inner rather than external attitudes.

Never doing a striptease. Keeping your dignity under all circumstances. Choosing your roles with care. Planning your future. And avoiding doing anything with the sole aim of catching public attention.

She said that although she had not succeeded in all her objectives, she did not regret her past. 'You know, when I look at my old photographs I don't find myself at all seductive. In fact I think I am far more beautiful today because I feel better balanced in myself and physically more mature. If I was twenty now, I should wait ten years before making a film!'

In her interview with *Paris Match* she took this theme further and said she thought forty-two was a 'nice age'.

'It is an age when one is no longer afraid. No longer afraid of other people's glances, no longer afraid of not always being thought the most beautiful person in the world. Obviously I hope I'm not a shrivelled old crone when I'm old, but I am far less afraid of growing old than I used to be. Do you know when I was nineteen I was terrified of the idea of being twenty-five. Today I have some white hairs, but I don't care. I don't dye them, in fact I think they are pretty. When you feel good, it is no longer so terrible to grow old. Personally, I feel like a rough diamond which has just been cut. I shine at last!'

Had she ever given any thoughts to retirement, she was asked. 'Perhaps when I'm fifty,' she said. 'Maybe I'll write or direct. It pains me to see some women valiantly playing character parts. It's all right to be mediocre when you're beginning a career, but not when you're reaching your zenith. Quit while you're ahead. When I lose my looks I'll get straight out of this racket. Are you kidding? Do you think I want to bust my gut like this for the rest of my life?' she laughed.

Raquel's year of happiness was rounded off perfectly when she announced that she and André were expecting a child the following August. It would mean, of course, that she would have to leave *Woman of the Year* at the end of her contract in January 1983, but she and her husband were delighted.

'We both talked about a child and wanted one,' André told journalists with a smile. 'I have never been a father and I am very excited. He will be a lion.'

212

'No,' said Raquel with an even broader grin, 'a lioness!' She continued: 'I'm so excited about having this baby and André is thrilled but I don't want to say too much. My kids are important to me, I'm proud of them all. Damon is now a college student and Tahnee wants to be an actress. We've always been extremely close, I never once used them for publicity to advance my career early on. They stayed well away from the public glare and as a result are good, strong, adjusted people. We're very close friends now and they're thrilled to bits because they know it's a wonderful time for me.'

On 2 January 1983 Raquel played her last full house at the Palace Theatre on Broadway and left the stage on a tide of emotion. It had been an exhausting, demanding but enormously exhilarating experience which had firmly established her as a genuinely accomplished actress. She had proved herself to be more than just a sex symbol and emerged a superstar. She had shown herself to be a star who could survive and succeed where others of her kind like Carole Landis, Jayne Mansfield and Marilyn Monroe had paid with their lives. Perhaps more than anything else she had revealed herself to be more than just a brainless, over-stacked body – but in actual fact a woman of rare intelligence, beautiful and talented into the bargain who had at last achieved her life's ambition.

She was, though, resigned to the fact that she would never completely escape from the sex symbol association, but she had come to terms with it. 'When you have the sex symbol image,' she ruminated to journalists before flying off to the island of Mustique for a well earned rest, 'you can't hate it, you can't love it, it's like your face being on Mount Rushmore – it just won't go away. I mean if you see Sophia Loren, you can think she's a fine dramatic actress, but your immediate reaction is that she's a beautiful and sexy woman. She will be called a sex symbol when she's eighty.

'I wasn't particularly unhappy with the sex goddess label. But it angered me the way some people tried to trivialise everything I did because of it. I know people say you created the monster so why complain? But the fact is I never really have complained. OK, whatever I do in my career, it will always be

''Raquel Welch, the sex symbol''. I don't kid myself about that. But I have no strong objections because it is part of my life, it's part of the image I helped to create. I know that if I were to do something like Shakespeare in the future, there will be someone who's more interested in my breasts than in my performance.'

She had, though, survived a great deal of smirking from critics before, and knew where her future lay. 'I know that being successful money-wise isn't the answer. And being successful in the eyes of a lot of other people isn't the answer either. I guess what I'm concerned with now is finding some kind of spontaneity in my life and work. I don't want to have to hedge my bets any more. I want to do something because it feels like a good idea, not because it's the right career decision. I just want to have a little fun.'

And for once, as Raquel headed off for the wide blue yonder of the Caribbean and into the fourth decade of her remarkable career, there was not a journalist who felt able to dispute a word she had said.

POSTSCRIPT: Unhappily, while on Mustique, Raquel suffered a miscarriage and despite being rushed to hospital, lost her baby. Shortly afterwards she and André returned to New York to continue their careers.

'The Dream Girl' – a beautiful portrait of Raquel

Filmography

ROUSTABOUT (1964)
Paramount Pictures. Produced by Hal B. Wallis; directed by John Rich. Screenplay by Anthony Lawrence, based on a story by Allan Weiss. Starring: Elvis Presley (Charlie), Barbara Stanwyck (Maggie), Joan Freeman (Cathy Lean), Leif Erickson (Joe Lean), Sue Anne Langdon (Madame Mijanou), Pat Buttram (Harry Caver), Diane Libby (Sexy Girl), Joe Forte (Concessionaire), Teri Hope, Linda Foster, Lynn Borden and Raquel Welch (College Students).

DO NOT DISTURB (1964)
20th Century-Fox. Produced by Aaron Rosenberg and Martin Melcher; directed by Ralph Levy. Screenplay by Milt Rosen and Richard Breen, based on a play by William Fairchild. Starring: Doris Day (Janet Harper), Rod Taylor (Mike Harper), Hermione Baddeley (Vanessa Courtwright), Sergio Fantoni (Paul Bellari), Reginald Gardiner (Simmons), Maura McGiveney (Claire Hackett), Raquel Welch (Young Woman).

A HOUSE IS NOT A HOME (1964)
Embassy Pictures. Produced by Clarence Greene; directed by Russell Rouse. Screenplay by Russell Rouse and Clarence Greene based on a book by Polly Adler. Starring: Shelley Winters (Polly Adler), Robert Taylor (Frank Costigan), Cesar Romero (Lucky Luciano), Ralph Taeger (Casey Booth), Kaye Ballard (Sidonia), Broderick Crawford (Harrigan), Mickey Shaughnessy (Sgt John Riordan), Sandra Grant, Diane Libby, Francine Pyne, Edy Williams, Raquel Welch (Polly's Girls).

A SWINGIN' SUMMER (1965)
United Screen World. Produced by Reno Carell; directed by Robert Sparr. Screenplay by Leigh Chapman, based on a story by Reno Carell. Starring: William Wellman (Rick), Quinn O'Hara (Cindy), James Stacy (Mickey), Martin West (Turk),

Raquel Welch (Jeri), Mary Mitchell (Shirley), The Righteous Brothers, Gary Lewis and the Playboys, The Rip Chords, Donnie Brooks and Jody Miller.

FANTASTIC VOYAGE (1966)

20th Century-Fox. Produced by Saul David; directed by Richard Fleischer. Screenplay by Harry Kleiner, based on a novel by Otto Klement and Jay Lewis Bixby. Starring: Stephen Boyd (Grant), Raquel Welch (Cora Peterson), Edmond O'Brien (General Carter), Donald Pleasance (Doctor Michaels), Arthur O'Connell (Col. Donald Reid), Arthur Kennedy (Doctor Duval), Ken Scott (Secret Service Man).

ONE MILLION YEARS BC (1966)

20th Century-Fox. Produced by Michael Carreras; directed by Don Chaffey. Screenplay by Michael Carreras, based on a story by Mickell Novak, George Baker and Joseph Frickert. Starring: John Richardson (Tumak), Raquel Welch (Loana), Percy Herbert (Sakana), Robert Brown (Akholba), Martine Beswick (Nupondi), Jean Waldon (Ahot), Lisa Thomas (Sura), Malya Nappi (Tohana), William Lyon Brown (Payto).

SHOUT LOUD, LOUDER, I DON'T UNDERSTAND

(1967) *(Spara Forte, Piu Forte . . . Non Capisco)*
Embassy Pictures. Executive Producer Joseph E. Levine; directed by Eduardo De Filippo. Screenplay by Eduardo De Filippo and Suso Cecchi D'Amico, based on the play *Le Voci di Dentro* by Eduardo De Filippo. Starring: Marcello Mastroianni (Alberto Saporito), Raquel Welch (Tania Mottini), Guido Alberti (Pasquale Cimmaruta), Leopoldo Trueste (Carlo Saporito), Eduardo De Filippo (Uncle Nicola), Rosalba Grottesi (Elvira Cimmaruta).

THE OLDEST PROFESSION (1967) *(Le Plus Vieux Metier Du Monde)*
Goldstone Pictures. Produced by Joseph Bergholz, 'The Gay Nineties' sequence directed by Michael Pfleghar. Screenplay by George and André Tabet. Starring; Raquel Welch (Nini) and Martin Held (Client).

SEX QUARTET (1967) *(Le Fate)*
Royal Films. Produced by Gianni Lucari, 'Queen Elena' sequence directed by Mauro Bolognini. Screenplay by Rodolfo Sonego. Starring: Raquel Welch (Elena), Jean Sorel (Luigi), Pia Lindstrom (Claudia), Massimo Forhari (Alberto).

THE BIGGEST BUNDLE OF THEM ALL (1967)
MGM Films. Produced by Josef Shaftel; directed by Ken Annakin. Screenplay by Josef Shaftel. Starring Vittorio De Sica (Cesare Celli), Raquel Welch (Juliana), Robert Wagner (Harry Price), Edward G. Robinson (Professor Samuels), Godfrey Cambridge (Benjamin Brownstead), Davy Kaye (Davey Collins), Victor Spinetti (Capt. Giglio), Mickey Knox (Joe Ware).

FATHOM (1967)
20th Century-Fox. Produced by John Kohn; directed by Leslie Martinson. Screenplay by Lorenzo Semple Jnr, based on a book by Larry Forester. Starring: Anthony Franciosa (Peter Merriweather), Raquel Welch (Fathom Harvill), Ronald Fraser (Douglas Campbell), Greta Chi (Jo-May Soon), Richard Briers (Timothy), Clive Revill (Serapkin), Tutta Lemkow (Mehmed).

BEDAZZLED (1967)
20th Century-Fox. Produced and directed by Stanley Donen. Screenplay by Peter Cook, based on a story by Peter Cook and Dudley Moore. Starring: Peter Cook (George Spiggot), Dudley

Moore (Stanley Moon), Eleanor Bron (Margaret), Raquel Welch (Lillian Lust), Barry Humphries (Envy), Howard Goorney (Sloth), Michael Bates (Inspector Clarke).

BANDOLERO! (1968)

20th Century-Fox. Produced by Robert L. Jacks; directed by Andrew V. McLaglen. Screenplay by James Lee Barrett, based on a story by Stanley L. Hough. Starring: James Stewart (Mace Bishop), Dean Martin (Dee Bishop), Raquel Welch (Maria Stoner), George Kennedy (Sheriff Johnson), Andrew Prine (Roscoe Bookbinder), Will Geer (Pop Chaney), Clint Ritchie (Babe).

LADY IN CEMENT (1968)

20th Century-Fox. Produced by Aaron Rosenberg; directed by Gordon Douglas. Screenplay by Marvin H. Albert and Jack Guss, based on a novel by Marvin H. Albert. Starring: Frank Sinatra (Tony Rome), Raquel Welch (Kitty Forrest), Richard Conte (Lt Santini), Martin Gabel (Al Munger), Lainie Kazan (Maria Baretto), Pat Henry (Rubin), Dan Blocker (Gronsky).

100 RIFLES (1969)

20th Century-Fox. Produced by Marvin Schwartz; directed by Tom Gries. Screenplay by Clair Huffaker, based on a novel by Robert MacLeod. Starring: Jim Brown (Lyedecker), Raquel Welch (Sarita), Burt Reynolds (Yaqui Joe), Fernando Lamas (General Verdugo), Dan O'Herlihy (Grimes), Hans Gudegast (von Klemme), Michael Forest (Humara), Aldo Sambrell (Sgt Paletes).

FLARE-UP (1969)

MGM Pictures. Produced by Leon Fromkess; directed by James Neilson. Screenplay by Mark Rodgers. Starring: Raquel Welch (Michele), James Stacy (Joe Brodnek), Luke Askew (Alan

Morris), Don Chastain (Lt Manion), Ron Rifkin ('Sailor'), Jeane Byron (Jerri Benton), Kay Peters (Lee), Pat Delany (Iris), Sandra Giles (Nikki).

THE MAGIC CHRISTIAN (1970)
Commonwealth United Pictures. Produced by Denis O'Dell; directed by Joseph McGrath. Screenplay by Terry Southern and Joseph McGrath from a novel by Terry Southern. Starring: Peter Sellers (Sir Guy Grand), Ringo Starr (Youngman Grand), Isabel Jeans and Caroline Blakiston (Sir Guy's Sisters), Wilfred Hyde-White (Ship's Capt.) and Guest Stars Richard Attenborough, Yul Brynner, Laurence Harvey, Christopher Lee, Spike Milligan, Roman Polanski and Raquel Welch.

THE BELOVED (1970)
MGM Pictures. Produced by Patrick Curtis; directed by George Pankosmotos. Screenplay by Michael Panyotis and George Pankosmotos. Starring: Raquel Welch (Elena), Richard Johnson (Orestes), Jack Hawkins (Le Prêtre), Frank Wolff (Alexis).

MYRA BRECKINRIDGE (1970)
20th Century-Fox. Produced by Robert Fryer; directed by Michael Sarne. Screenplay by Michael Sarne and David Giler from the novel by Gore Vidal. Starring: Raquel Welch (Myra Breckinridge), Rex Reed (Myron Breckinridge), Mae West (Leticia Van Allen), John Huston (Buck Loner), Farrah Fawcett (Mary Ann), Roger C. Carmel (Dr Montag), Roger Herren (Rusty), Calvin Lockhart (Irving Amadeus), Jim Backus (Doctor), John Carradine (Surgeon), Genevieve Gilles (Patient).

HANNIE CAULDER (1971)
Tigon Pictures. Executive Producer David Haft; directed by Burt Kennedy. Screenplay by Z. X. Jones. Starring: Raquel

Welch (Hannie Caulder), Robert Culp (Thomas Luther Price), Ernest Borgnine (Emmet Clemens), Jack Elam (Frank Clemens), Strother Martin (Rufus Clemens).

FUZZ (1971)
United Artists. Produced by Jack Farren; directed by Richard A. Colla. Screenplay by Evan Hunter, based on the novel by Ed McBain. Starring: Burt Reynolds (Det. Steve Carella), Raquel Welch (Det. Eileen McHenry), Jack Weston (Det. Meyer Meyer), Tom Skerritt (Det. Bert King), James McEachin (Det. Arthur Brown), Steve Ihnat (Det. Andy Parker), Dan Frazer (Lt Byrnes), Yul Brynner (The Deaf Man).

BLUEBEARD (1971)
Cinerama Releasing Ltd. Produced by Alexander Salkind; directed by Edward Dmytryk. Screenplay by Ennio Di Concini, Edward Dmytryk and Maria Pia Fusco. Starring: Richard Burton (Bluebeard), Raquel Welch (Magdalena), Joey Heatherton (Anne), Virna Lisi (Elga), Nathalie Delon (Erika), Marilu Tolo (Brigitte), Karin Schubert (Greta), Agostina Belli (Caroline), Sybil Danning (The Prostitute), Edward Meeks (Sergio).

KANSAS CITY BOMBER (1972)
MGM Films. Produced by Marty Elfand; directed by Jerrold Freedman. Screenplay by Thomas Rickman and Calvin Clements, based on a story by Barry Sandler. Starring: Raquel Welch (K. C. Carr), Kevin McCarthy (Burt Henry), Helena Kallianiotes (Jackie Burdette), Norman Alden (Horrible Hank Hopkins), Jeanne Cooper (Vivien), Mary Kay Pass (Lovely), Martine Bartlett (Mrs Carr), Stephen Manley (Walt Carr), Jodie Foster (Rita Carr).

THE LAST OF SHEILA (1972)
Warner Bros. Produced and directed by Herbert Ross. Screenplay by Stephen Sondheim and Anthony Perkins. Starring: Richard Benjamin (Tom), Dyan Cannon (Christine), James Coburn (Clinton), Joan Hackett (Lee), James Mason (Philip), Ian McShane (Anthony), Raquel Welch (Alice), Yvonne Romaine (Sheila).

THE THREE MUSKETEERS (*The Queen's Diamonds*) (1973)
20th Century-Fox. Produced by Alexander Salkind; directed by Richard Lester. Screenplay by George MacDonald Fraser, based on the novel by Alexander Dumas. Starring: Oliver Reed (Athos), Raquel Welch (Mme Bonancieux), Richard Chamberlain (Aramis), Frank Finlay (Porthos), Christopher Lee (Rochefort), Geraldine Chaplin (Anne of Austria), Jean Pierre Cassel (Louis XIII), Spike Milligan (M Bonancieux), Sybil Danning (Eugenie), Faye Dunaway (Milady), Charlton Heston (Cardinal Richelieu).

THE FOUR MUSKETEERS (*The Revenge of Milady*) (1974)
20th Century-Fox. Produced by Alexander Salkind; directed by Richard Lester. Screenplay by George MacDonald Fraser, based on the novel by Alexander Dumas. Starring: Oliver Reed (Athos), Raquel Welch (Mme Bonancieux), Richard Chamberlain (Aramis), Michael York (D'Artagnan), Frank Finlay (Porthos), Christopher Lee (Rochefort), Geraldine Chaplin (Anne of Austria), Simon Ward (Buckingham), Faye Dunaway (Milady), Charlton Heston (Cardinal Richelieu).

THE WILD PARTY (1975)
American International Pictures. Produced by Ismail Merchant; directed by James Ivory. Screenplay by Walter Marks, based on a narrative poem by Joseph Moncure March. Starring: James Coco (Jolly Grimm), Raquel Welch (Queenie), Perry King (Dale Sword), Tiffany Bolling (Kate), Royal Dano

(Tex), David Dukes (James Morrison), Dena Dietrich (Mrs Murchison), Regis J. Cordic (Mr Murchison), Bobo Lewis (Wilma).

MOTHER, JUGS AND SPEED (1976)

20th Century-Fox. Produced by Peter Yates and Tom Mankiewicz; directed by Peter Yates. Screenplay by Tom Mankiewicz, based on a story by Stephen Manes and Tom Mankiewicz. Starring: Bill Cosby (Orlin 'Mother' Tucker), Raquel Welch (Jennifer 'Jugs' Jurgens), Harvey Keitel (Tony 'Speed' Malatesta), Allen Garfield (Harry Fishbine), Dick Butkus (Rodeo), L. Q. Jones (Davey Walker), Bruce Davison (Leroy Watkins), Larry Hagman (John Murdoch), Toni Basil (Drug Addict).

THE PRINCE AND THE PAUPER (1976)

20th Century-Fox. Produced by Ilya Salkind; directed by Richard Fleischer. Screenplay by Berta Dominguez, Pierre Spengler and George MacDonald Fraser, based on the novel by Mark Twain. Starring: Oliver Reed (Miles Hendon), Raquel Welch (Edith), Mark Lester (Tom Canty/Prince Edward), Ernest Borgnine (John Canty), George C. Scott (The Ruffler), Rex Harrison (Duke of Norfolk), David Hemmings (Hugh Hendon), Charlton Heston (Henry VIII), Harry Andrews (Duke of Hertford), Sybil Danning (Mother Canty), Lalla Ward (Princess Elizabeth).

L'ANIMAL (1977)

RFC Films. Produced and directed by Claude Zizi. Screenplay by Michel Audiard. Starring: Jean-Paul Belmondo, Raquel Welch, Dany Saval, Raymond Gérôme, Charles Gérard.

THE LEGEND OF WALKS FAR WOMAN (1979)

NBC TV. Produced and directed by Mel Damski. Screenplay by Evan Hunter from a novel by Colin Stuart. Starring: Raquel Welch.